ENDORSEMENTS

Pastors need pastors, and Dr. Bob Rhoden has been a pastor to me for twenty-five years. Everybody needs somebody who sees more potential in them than they see in themselves. Bob Rhoden has been that person for me. I'm eternally grateful for his wisdom, his faith, and his grace in my life. Wherever you are in your spiritual journey FROM and TO, this book will help you take the next step!

—Mark Batterson, Author and Pastor of
National Community Church, Washington, DC

How many people could write an autobiography of their long life without glossing over at least a few incidents, if not leaving them out altogether? I have no doubt that Bob Rhoden—whom I've known since we were in our mid-20s—has in this book given us the literal truth, from his earliest days as a barefoot kid in his grandmother's cottage near the railroad tracks with no electricity or indoor plumbing, to planting a church that still thrives, to giving regional and national leadership to his denomination, to wisely mentoring dozens of younger ministers. He is a clear modern example of what Jesus said about his disciple Nathanael—"Behold an Israelite indeed, in whom is no guile!" (John 1:47). Read this book, and see if I'm right.

—Dean Merrill, award-winning author/collaborator and editor
(*Campus Life, Leadership Journal, Christian Herald,*
the Focus on the Family magazine group)

Restless to Reconciled reminds us that our future is not predetermined by our past. Bob's story is a testament to this. He understands that hope is the vehicle that drives us into our divinely designed future. Whether you are on a mountain or in a valley, you must read this journey of hope! This book is a gift from God to empower your life with purpose, meaning, and significance.

—Kent J. Ingle | President, Southeastern University

Doc Rhoden has done it again. He has captured highlights from his life experiences, and in writing, presents them as a resource to help you focus on where you are going, keeping in mind that our steps really are ordered by the Lord. *From Restless To Reconciled* is a journey to help you understand that you are God's workmanship, created in Christ Himself to do good things that He has prepared. Enjoy the read!

—Doug Clay, General Superintendent of the Assemblies of God

Dr Bob Rhoden has been a friend of mine for six decades. Please don't presume anything, because he's a very young man. His whole life has been about NEXT. The reason I love this book he's written is because this is the first time I've known Dr Rhoden to pause in order to look back. I'm so glad he did. His personal history is a page turner of divine grace. Please do everything possible to get your five closest friends to read it as well. I'm still blessed when I think of this wonderful read..."From Restless To Reconciled"

—Rich Wilkerson, Pastor, Trinity Church, Miami, Fl.

This is such an inspiring account of how God can take brokenness and turn it into triumph. As Pastor Bob shares his experiences, there are so many principles that we can learn about LIFE. This is a must read for all Pastors seeking to lead God's people.

—Bishop Daniel Robertson, Jr.
Mt. Gilead Full Gospel International Ministries
North Chesterfield, VA

Get ready for a feel-good story. A journey of hope from a boy with a tragically humbled beginning to a man with influence around the world. We are indeed blessed that Dr. Robert Rhoden has shared his story with us. You will be encouraged and inspired. A must read for those who are looking for motivation for their own journey.

—Frank Potter, Superintendent, Potomac Ministry Network

Tracing a life on its journey between "from" and "to" gives opportunity for reflection about what it means to be human in the care of a holy love. Those who know my friend, Bob Rhoden, as a wise and widely-respected ministry leader may not know his remarkable back story, one which weaves a rich personal journey of growth, faith, and becoming into a sturdy, yet beautiful, tapestry of hope. If you're ready for a double dose of encouragement and inspiration, From Restless to Reconciled is your next delightful and important read!

—Dr. Jodi Detrick, Author of The Jesus-Hearted Woman:
10 Leadership Qualities for Enduring & Endearing Influence

Have you ever wondered if God can used you? Do you struggle with your past? After you read "Restless to Reconciled", you'll have a new perspective on God's plan for your life and future. You'll be encouraged and inspired to believe God for greater things!

—Rod Loy, Pastor, First Assembly of God, North Little Rock, AR

from RESTLESS *to* RECONCILED

---One Man's Journey---

BOB RHODEN

WITH J.B. RHODEN NICHOLAS

FREILING
PUBLISHING

Published by Freiling Publishing, a division of Freiling Agency, LLC.

P.O. Box 1264,
Warrenton, VA 20188

www.FreilingPublishing.com

ISBN 978-1-950948-36-9

Printed in the United States of America

TABLE OF CONTENTS

TABLE OF CONTENTS

FOREWORD

I first met Bob Rhoden in Illinois in November of 1966. We had grown up a continent apart. He in Olustee, Florida and I in east Oakland, California.

He graduated from a Bible college in Toccoa Falls, Georgia. I from one near Santa Cruz, California.

We both went to Wheaton College Graduate School in the 1960s and went on to be church planters. He in Richmond, Virginia and I in Urbana, Illinois.

Three decades later, we would re-connect in Washington D.C., where he would be an exceptional leader of many pastors and congregations. And, in my role, working behind the scenes personally with national leaders in government and business, Bob would be my colleague, counselor, and confidante. I would report to him and his team of leaders annually and he would always encourage me to "do the next thing."

I have been with him in scores of settings and with thousands of people from Illinois to Prince Edward Island, Canada, from Washington, D.C. to Chennai, South India.

I've watched and listened. He has never wavered.

Always wise. Always encouraging.

Always bringing hope.

Always proclaiming Jesus.

I would trust him with my life.

He is my dear friend.

That he would write his story now is a wonderful gift to all of us. It is way more than a rags-to-riches tale. It is a deeply moving account that takes us from "not-much-chance-at-all" to "let's-touch-the-whole-world."

With his daughter, Julie, Bob stitches a colorful quilt that wraps the reader in pictures, emotions and dreams. I predict you will find yourself in one of those "patches" that makes the whole so rich and vibrant.

The pieces of Bob's journey, in his own reflections, have been stitched together by the grace of God. In the most unlikely moments and most unlikely places. In times of great elation and times of deep despair. That grace balanced by truth has held him.

And, not too far into his journey, we get to meet Joan, the love of Bob's life. At the risk of putting too much weight on the metaphor, it is in that relationship that Bob's quilt gets its "backing." Joan, my Ruth's dear friend, is a "just right" match and inspiration. What a team they are!

If I was asked to describe my friend, Bob, in a word, the answer would be instant: HOPE. He can start anywhere in the Scriptures and end up at **hope**. Walking with people through their catastrophes, he will take them to **hope**. Talking with grandchildren, **hope** will always be in play. I think that's a key reason that I love being with him. I walk away encouraged by **hope.**

You'll see it when you read this book. For a little boy living with his Grandma in uncertain times, who didn't know who or where his dad was, "Bit by bit, hope slipped under the door and through the cracks in the little Olustee place, we called home."

Let Bob's journey give meaning to yours!

Dick Foth
Windsor, Colorado
August 1, 2020

HOPE FOR THE JOURNEY

"Where are you from?"

This is a common question when we meet someone for the first time. I've probably asked and answered this in hundreds of conversations over a lifetime. George Ella Lyon answers this question beautifully in her poem, *Where I'm From*. The descriptive language and cadence sweep us into her past and allow us to see her, really see her.

> *"I'm from the know-it-alls*
>
> *and the pass-it-ons,*
>
> *from Perk up! and Pipe down!*
>
> *I'm from He restoreth my soul*
>
> *with a cottonball lamb*
>
> *and ten verses I can say myself."*

The poem is also a thoughtful invitation to consider where we are each from. Which people, places, and memories shape us? When our grandson, Brennan, was in middle school he wrote his personal version of this classic poem.

WHERE I'M FROM
BY BRENNAN GAGNON

I am from a skateboard, the X-Box 360 and Honey Bunches of Oats.
From the homey, welcoming, grey painted house on 11 Summit Road,
and the green, freshly mowed lawn.

I am from southern New Hampshire and the blueberry bush.
From Sunday brunch, memere's muffins, and quiche.
I am from blond and brown, fair and tan.

I am from Phyllis, Roland, and all of the Rhodens.
From southern hospitality and New England pride.
I am from the focus and drive of athletes
And the patience and compassion of educators.

I am from "I'm proud of you" and "Always try your hardest."
From The Lord's Prayer and many bible verses,the humble manger
and the Cross.

I am from the time my aunt was diagnosed with Crohn's,
and when my uncle tore his ACL.
From old dusty boxes in the basement,
boxes that are scarcely touched.
Boxes passed down through the family,
And boxes with memories that I will never forget.

The poem started out as an assignment, but ended up framed, sitting on a nightstand in our home. My wife and I thought he was the most brilliant kid in the world, as most grandparents do with their grandchildren. Over the years, those words and the details of his poem stirred my own thoughts. What would my version of the poem, *Where I'm From* say?

One morning, as I was reading the Gospel of John, I noticed that Nathanael made a sarcastic comment to Philip. *"Nazareth! Can anything good come from there?"* (John 1:46). A question others might have thought, but not spoken. Nazareth was a small, poor village, nestled in the hills near the Sea of Galilee. Its underwhelming population of 400 hardly noticed Jesus' birth and all the scandal surrounding it. This insignificant hometown followed Jesus all the way to the cross, where Pilate's crudely written sign declared for all to see, *"Jesus of Nazareth, the King of the Jews"* (John 19:19).

As I reflected on who I am and where I'm from, another question formed inside me - where am I going? My story starts with "from," but it certainly doesn't end there. In John 13:36 Peter asks Jesus, *"Lord, where are you going?"* Jesus and his disciples have eaten a passover meal and Jesus shares that he won't be with them much longer. He also says they can't come with him to this place. At least not yet. When Peter asks where he is going, Jesus answers by saying again that Peter can't come with him now, but later. Jesus had a "from," but he also had a "to." His "to" was much more than any of his disciples could imagine or believe.

From Restless To Reconciled embraces the idea that our past does not have to trap us, it can shape us. We were created to journey forward. To focus on where we are going. To make choices and trust God's direction in our "to." We acknowledge our "from," but we live in our "to." So here is my story. Come with me and let's explore hope for the journey!

FROM

1
ARRIVING

"Jesus help us. Show us the way."

It would be nice if our "from" arrived in a neat, tidy package. Maybe wrapped with a crisp bow; a fragrant sprig of evergreen peeking out from underneath. Something we could carry around with pride. But for many this is not the case. Our "from" comes in all shapes and sizes. It's bent at the corners. Torn and messy. Unpredictable. Some look pretty hopeless.

In 1942 Martha Lee Cobb was a teen-aged Baker County girl, daughter of Florence Cobb. She was the youngest of seven and lived on a meager farm outside Sanderson, Florida with her mother and a few farm hands. Her father had passed away a few years before, and all her siblings were grown and out of the house.

Martha was drawn to a young man who worked as a farm hand for her family. He worked long, hot days and enjoyed the way Martha, although young, could talk about anything with her cool, flirty voice. Baker County was known back in those days for moonshine and gambling. Evenings and weekends were for hanging out and dancing around trouble. Years later when I heard the story of my mom and dad told in hushed voices, there were gaps and unexplained silences I never understood. I did understand that my mom was fourteen and unmarried when she became pregnant. I understood she and her mom lived alone on a small farm in a rural town with limited means. I understood my story was not one of a hopeful beginning. A baby having a baby. A small town scandal. An unknown future. Not the neat and tidy package we long for. Good thing hope isn't limited to packaging.

Folks whispered and gossiped as Martha Lee's dresses grew tighter around her waist. Who was the father? How far along was she? What kind of daughter had Florence raised? How was a young girl going to provide for a child when she was still a child herself? This whispered sin hung heavy as a wool blanket in the thick summer air. Mother and daughter sat on the porch each evening just waiting and hoping for answers to blow in on a cool breeze.

Fear. Worry. Shame. These threatened to suffocate and paralyze hope in the dark of night, but when carefully examined and held up to the light of a new day, the faintest shimmer of possibility appeared forcing everything else back into the shadows for a while. My granny, Florence, knew a name with greater power than any troubles on earth. I imagine early before daylight stirred or late when all was quiet, she lifted her troubles up to the light and pleaded, "Jesus, help us. Show us the way." Wisdom. Provision. Understanding. These were her requests.

Harold Rhoden agreed to marry my mom, Martha Lee, and give me a respectable name. On October 14, 1942 I entered this world as Harold Robert Rhoden. My mother was a few days shy of fifteen. We all lived on the farm - me, Martha Lee, and Florence. There were long nights when I didn't sleep or just wanted to be held after I was fed and changed. Time flew by in a blur of bottles, diapers, naps, and new discoveries. Chores and decisions connected with farm life filled the days, weaving between and around all of the new baby responsibilities.

Unfortunately, even with the extra help from Granny, navigating married life and caring for a new baby proved too difficult for my young parents. Harold and Martha Lee divorced within a year. I wasn't old enough to understand or even store a memory of the only father I ever knew. Harold gave me his name, but it would be years before we saw each other again. By then, I would be a completely different person.

2
MOVING

"...ba-ba-ba-ba"

Granny Cobb decided her family needed a change. With a heavy heart, she sold the farm to her sons and they helped move her to Olustee, another small Florida town closer to family. A new place. A fresh start. Surely, things would grow easier again soon.

Over the next year, bit by bit, hope slipped in under the door and through the cracks in the little Olustee place we called home. I learned to walk and speak my first words. My mother learned to care for me as I grew. Granny made a life for herself and her family in a new town. Joyful moments filled the home. A young diaper-clad boy toddled on wobbly legs through the chickens, chasing them and screaming, "ba-ba-ba-ba," with delight as they squawked and flapped away from him. A girl danced around the front room and swooped up her baby boy to join her in the skirt-twirling rhythms. A family of three, representing three generations, picnicked in the front yard. These new light-dappled moments fluttered in and filled our Olustee home, pushing out the old, dark memories that still lurked in quiet corners.

By the time another October arrived, Martha Lee had fallen for a man in uniform, Ashley Weeks. Ashley was handsome, dependable, loved me, and quickly became a familiar face in our home. Granny wasn't surprised when he asked Martha Lee to marry him. Ashley was only two years older than Martha Lee, but promised with all his heart to take care of all of us. He even requested adoption papers to ensure that I would officially become his son.

One winter evening Martha and Ashley walked into town planning to have a fun evening of dinner and dancing at a local establishment. Ashley was in the Navy and home on leave. They were newly married and in love. I was two years old and safe at home with Granny. Granny must have felt like life was finally starting to settle into something more manageable. As the lovers walked along the narrow, two-lane road, maybe they talked about what they were going to eat or how long they were going to dance. My mom was newly pregnant, so perhaps they dreamt about the future and whether I was going to have a new little brother or sister. Maybe they discussed names for the baby or playfully argued over when they should move out of Granny's house to build a life on their own. Whatever they were discussing or thinking about was lost forever when a drunk driver carelessly swerved off the road and crashed into Ashley and my mother, killing them instantly. Young, hopeful lives snuffed out in a split-second. There was no warning. There was no time for last minute goodbyes. They were just ... gone.

I don't remember the commotion to follow or the funeral or the unimaginable sadness that must have settled into every day for months afterward. Granny and I were left to figure out the future together, two people at complete opposite ends of life. What lay ahead for us? Could joy ever bloom again? Could Granny's God - the God she trusted with her hopes and dreams, the God she trusted with her fourteen-year-old unwed pregnant daughter, the God she trusted with giving up the farm and leaving a home she'd loved - could this God still be trusted to pick up the pieces with us now that everything we loved was gone? Could He be trusted to bear the heavy weight of loss with us? Could He be trusted to provide for our future?

I was too young to believe in God, but Granny believed for the both of us. She knew God held us in the commotion that followed. She knew He mourned with us at the funeral and sat with us as the unimaginable sadness settled into every day for months afterward. She prayed God was diligently and quietly working on our behalf as He always had, even when it was hard to believe. We couldn't have known that while our hearts were trying to heal, adoption documents Ashley signed days earlier were being processed and already creating a way for our hopeful future.

3
RESPECTS

"Bobby, we need to have a talk about..."

Granny Cobb was once again left to pick up the pieces of a broken story. The sadness of losing my mother and the reality of caring for me must have been overwhelming. With a limp from rheumatoid arthritis and a weariness from hard physical labor combined with deep heartache, Granny moved through each day with determination. She had raised seven children and figured out how to run a farm after my grandfather died. She knew that alongside food, clothing, and shelter, I also needed love, nurture, and stability. She didn't have much, but she had what mattered. She also had the help of her grown children and some of her extended family living close by.

I grew into a youngster quickly and found all sorts of places to explore in Olustee. Granny was clever and strict, but she knew that her tired bones were no match for a strong-willed, energetic, barefoot Florida-boy like me. I didn't much care for rules, and certainly didn't care for chores, but I loved Granny dearly. Being a quick learner, I figured out early in life that if I followed Granny's four r's, she was content and rewarded me with lots of freedom. Her four r's were: respect for self, respect for authority, respect for property, and respect for time.

My tension as a youngster did not come from understanding the four r's but from trying to sort out cultural church rules my grandmother embraced. I wasn't allowed to attend movies or dance or play the pinball machine like most of my friends. I did sneak around and play a pinball machine a couple of times despite the strong guilt, but never saw movies or danced until my teen years when we moved to Jacksonville. I knew it would hurt Granny and make her cry if I violated any of these cultural church rules or her four r's. It was her deep love for me that guided her in teaching me about life. I loved Granny, so I wanted to be compliant; but sometimes my curiosity got the best of me.

Granny had a stellar reputation around the community. People knew it was a challenge for her to keep the reins on me, so they became her "village" to help keep me in line with her guidelines. Even when I didn't agree or understand, I never went to sleep wondering if I was loved. I was loved deeply. Granny's words were comforting and full of faith, "Bobby, I love you and God loves you. Always follow God."

When Granny started a sentence with "Bobby, we need to have a talk about …," it usually had to do with one of the respects. Even though there were only four to remember, these respects efficiently covered every area of life and kept me out of more trouble than I probably realized. However, I had some tough lessons learning to understand Granny's four r's and how they applied to my daily life.

4
SELF

"Don't forget to scrub behind your ears Bobby!"

Every Saturday night was bath night. Granny filled the #10 wash tub with hot water in the backyard for us to get "cleaned up" for church the next morning.

"Yes, Granny," came my reluctant answer.

"And those other parts," she called through the window.

"I know, Granny," I sighed.

"Taking care of yourself. . .," she started.

". . . is part of the first respect, respect for self," I finished.

Granny nodded triumphantly.

Boy and bath water have always had a close relationship. Boy plays with water; water cleans boy. I knew just how hard to squeeze a bar of soap sending it straight up in the air like a ball shooting from a canon. I discovered wet armpits created the most glorious sound when you cupped a hand under one and flapped your arm like a chicken wing. By the time I finished my bath there was usually more water outside the tub than inside, but somehow all the dirt from a week's worth of living slipped off in the hot water and I emerged clean. Fresh skin squeaked between my toes and elbow creases. Nails shone. Freckles sparkled. After passing Granny's inspection and helping refill the tub, I had time to daydream or build a small toy from scraps of wood while Granny took her turn.

Granny also scrubbed laundry in the #10 wash tub. She pushed clothes up and down on a wood and glass washboard until not a speck or stain remained. She made sure I had clean shirts even though they were simple and hand-sewn from flour sacks. She ordered pants from the Sears Roebuck Catalog. Shoes, however, were not a necessity for most of the year in rural Florida in the 40's. Tough feet served the same purpose and were far more economical.

Respect for self was the first of Granny's four respects. I can still hear her words in my head, "Bobby, if you don't have respect for yourself, how can you have respect for anything else?"

5
PROPERTY

"We need to take care of what we have."

Chores have been the bane of a young boy's life for as long as recorded time. I had chores. Lots of chores. I gathered eggs from the hen house, cleaned the ashes from the fireplace, fed the animals, weeded the garden and more. Each day required these jobs to maintain the house and keep our property and possessions in order. Granny used to say, "Bobby, you have to respect property. I can't afford to replace everything. We need to take care of what we have."

One day my cousin, Richard came to visit for the afternoon. We decided to explore the backyard and find something to do. As we approached the edge of the yard, I noticed that one of the hens had made a strange place to lay her eggs. Instead of using the hen house, she laid eggs in a corner of the yard and left them to rot. Rotten eggs sitting in my very own backyard! Fully whole, fully unclaimed. These eggs were taunting, even begging two young boys to pick them up and let the mischief begin. Richard and I held these smooth, stench-filled ovals in our eager hands. We said nothing, but imagined everything. What would it feel like to smash one? What would it smell like? How would it sound?

Without a word, we grabbed the eggs and snuck behind the smokehouse where Granny couldn't see us. I looked at Richard and raised one eyebrow in a question. With a look of both fear and excitement, he slowly gave me the nod of approval. That was all I needed. I took the stance of my favorite major league pitcher, Allie Reynolds, paused, moved through the wind-up, and beamed the first rotten egg toward home plate. It was a fast strike in motion and made a satisfying SPLAT! when the egg cracked open against the side of the smokehouse and dripped down the tin siding leaving a slimy trail that stunk to the high heavens. I looked over at Richard who was pinching his nose and said, "P.U.!" We both cracked up.

Before long, all the rotten eggs flew through the air one at a time.The splat and instant odor became a kind of familiar pattern that thrilled us and brought instant gratification. When the eggs were gone, we stood back in wonder at our fine work until the awful truth settled in our bones. Granny was going to tan our hides.

I spent hours scrubbing rotten eggs off the side of the smokehouse. Hours with the stench of sulfur inside my nose and the sting of a proper whipping across my backside. Hours pondering Granny's respects, with one in particular rising above all the others - respect for property.

6
TIME

"Please don't be late," she called after us.

Everyone knew about the third grade field trip to Silver Springs. Silver Springs was a state park in Ocala, Florida filled with nature and animal exhibits. While the animal exhibits were interesting, the glass-bottomed boat rides were the highlight everyone talked about. The glass floor on the boat provided a window for peeking at life beneath the surface of the water. Fish, turtles, alligators, and many other kinds of Floridian, swampy wildlife swam in perfect view beneath your feet. Not to mention the flora, although that was too boring for an adventurous boy like me.

The day finally arrived and I could hardly wait as I walked to school. After the hour and a half bus ride, we poured out into the parking lot like one organism of wiggling, squirming cells. Even our teacher was excited and energetic. She gave clear instructions about staying together and paying attention to the time. We had the morning to explore and look at all the animal exhibits, but were to meet back at the boat dock for our scheduled boat ride at noon. I jiggled back and forth anxious to move. I had things to see! Then she set us loose.

"Please don't be late," she called after us. "The boat will leave on time and if you miss it, you will not get another chance to ride it." We spread out in different directions, nodding our heads like we were listening. Granny and I didn't have a car or much extra money to visit places like Silver Springs, so I was very curious about everything in the park. We saw lizards, birds, alligators, and my favorite, snakes. We ate our packed lunches and traded stories about all the cool sites we had seen so far. After lunch we had twenty minutes to finish looking before the boat ride. I went back to look at the snakes. They both terrified and mesmerized me. After a while I began to look around for my classmates and get ready for the boat ride. I couldn't find anyone, but figured maybe they were already by the boat dock. *I better hurry*, I thought to myself.

By the time I reached the dock, a sick feeling stirred in the pit of my stomach. Looking out across the water, I stared unbelievingly at the glass-bottomed boat moving away from the dock with the rest of my class on it. They had started the tour without me. I jumped up and down, waving my arms and yelling, "Wait! Wait for me!" But even as I yelled, I knew. They were not coming back. It was too late. I had missed it. I had lost track of time and missed the boat ride. I stood on the end of the dock with tears streaming down my face. The one thing I waited for all day at Silver Springs, and now I was too late! Watching that boat glide through the water without me was a painful lesson in understanding Granny's respect for time. I was shocked at how personal the consequence felt. It would be years before I went back to the park on my own as a young adult and rode the special boat.

In a similar situation, a few years later, I gained a new understanding of respecting time. The high school basketball team in Sanderson, near Olustee, made it to the playoffs and I begged to go and watch the game which was being held in another nearby town, Macclenny. Granny finally agreed to let me take a bus on a Friday night with some older kids to watch the game, and I promised to stay with the group the whole night. I sat in the bleachers with my friend, Charles, and cheered as the fast-paced competition on the court unfolded like a shoot-out scene from the Wild West. Both teams were well-matched and played hard, but Sanderson lost. The atmosphere in the gym was electrifying and the crowd's excitement so contagious that it easily pulled me into the next game between different schools.

It wasn't until much later in the evening that Charles and I realized we had missed the bus ride back to Olustee. Once again, time had slipped away from me. Luckily Charles had some relatives in Macclenny so we walked to their house and they gave us a ride back to Olustee. But it was very late, and there was no way to call Granny. We didn't even have a phone at home. Granny was worried sick about me when I hadn't showed up on the return bus, and was waiting up for me when I arrived home. She hugged me tight and said, "Bobby, where were you? I was so worried. I didn't know where you were or what had happened to you." I was ashamed and sad I had upset Granny. I realized that losing track of time not only brought consequences on myself, but sometimes on others I loved and cared about. Respect for time was hard for me to grasp and even harder to practice, but I finally understood the old saying, "Time waits for no one."

7
AUTHORITY

"Your Granny loves you very much and she is going to take care of everything."

Mrs. Dobson was my first teacher. Actually, she was everyone's first teacher in Olustee. Our town was so small that we only had one tiny elementary school and many of the classes were combined. Mrs. Dobson was the first/second grade teacher and divided her time between children ranging from ages five to seven in the same classroom. Everyone knew Mrs. Dobson and it was practically a rite of passage to have her as your teacher. She wore her graying hair styled in waves framing her face and displayed a classy sense of fashion. Her personality was nurturing and she always had an encouraging word for her students.

Mrs. Dobson was one of the first people in my life who had authority over me outside of family. Granny always insisted on respect for authority, and Mrs. Dobson was such a town icon that something about her just made you respect her without hardly trying. We respected her because of the way she treated others and wanted the best for her students no matter what kind of background we carried. Before I ever understood the whole complicated story about my mother and father, Mrs. Dobson would sometimes hug me and say, "Don't you worry, Bobby. Your Granny loves you very much and she is going to take care of everything." Her words brought me comfort and helped me foster a healthy trust and respect for authority.

In the classroom Mrs. Dobson's word held, but outside the classroom there was another authority we all respected, the authority of collective agreement. Even though the teachers supervised recess, we all knew and collectively agreed that Gene was in charge of kickball or anything else we played. If Gene said you were out, you were out! If Gene said something wasn't fair, that was the final word. He was never mean. He never tried to bully us. It's just that collectively, without ever discussing it, we made him our leader. And he led.

During the years I had Mrs. Dobson there was also a ghost mystery that circulated for a while among the students. In one of the larger classrooms that served as an activities room for gatherings like assemblies, there was a hole in the corner of the ceiling. This hole was about three feet in diameter and provided a dark, gaping abyss for young children to wonder about. The story we believed was that one afternoon someone had seen a strange pair of eyes looking out at them from the hole. That was all it took. It wasn't a question of who the eyes belonged to? We all knew it had to be a ghost. Plain and simple. The real question was were you brave enough to run into the room, stare into the hole, and look for the ghost eyes?

When I told Granny, she chuckled and said, "Bobby, there's no such thing as a ghost. That's just silly!" I didn't argue, but I knew she was wrong. I also knew the ghost roamed the school building at night hoping to capture any lone student who might be hanging around nearby. Everyone knew not to go near the school at night. One day my buddies, Melvin, Jack, and I decided to brave the room on a teacher's work day. Quietly we tiptoed past the teachers and slipped into the room. I don't remember which of us screamed and said, "I see him!" first, but all three of us scrambled to get out of there fast. We barely made it out alive!

I'm not exactly sure how the story faded away. Maybe someone fixed the hole. Maybe we decided the ghost had moved on to haunt a new place. Maybe a better mystery came along for us. Eventually the ghost-in-the-hole story ended and school life returned to normal. I'm sure the teachers got a kick out of our imaginations. Most of the time, Mrs. Dobson had our complete respect. But if she ever asked about the hole in the ceiling, we just pressed our lips together and shifted our eyes around like we didn't know what she was talking about. We had escaped the grip of the ghost. And we wanted to keep it that way!

8
COMFORT

"Bobby, we're gettin' electricity."

Comfort is something we learn at an early age. We learn by receiving it when we are upset or hurt. We learn from watching others give it. We even learn from the absence of comfort in our lives. In its absence we begin practicing how to comfort ourselves.

When I was very young, I loved to rock back and forth in a small rocking chair that was just my size. Sometimes I sat in front of the fireplace with a book in my lap and tried to read the pages. Back and forth. Back and forth. One evening I rocked forward too hard and fell out of the chair and onto the hearth. I threw my hands in front of me to catch myself. This saved my face from hitting the hot ashes of the fire, but placed the palms of my small hands in direct contact with the heat.

I cried out and Granny was there in an instant, full of comfort and care. She sliced a raw potato, lined my red, burned palms with the cool white ovals, and gently wrapped bandages around each hand to keep the potatoes in place. It was a long night. Anyone who has been through an accident or any kind of sickness with a young child knows that comfort is hard work and can feel endless and exhausting. But many times comfort is all we have to offer. My palms healed and never even scarred. The little rocking chair still sits in our home as a tribute to the care and comfort Granny provided in my life.

Sometimes Granny needed comforting. When she seemed tired or looked like she had been crying, I would ask her if we could sit on the couch. Then I'd lay my head in her lap, look up at her face and ask, "What's wrong? What can I do for you?" Granny's reply was always, "It will be alright Bobby. Your granny just has a lot on her mind." As a kid I never knew what to say or do. But maybe taking a few moments together made the difference. Maybe speaking the concern out loud was enough. In this small way I learned how to practice comfort among family first.

As I grew older, Granny taught me about comfort in other ways without realizing it. We didn't have much money or many possessions, but that was no excuse for being messy or dirty. At least that's what Granny thought! Our little home was always swept and scrubbed cleaner than clean. Granny sewed our clothes, patched the rips and tears, and ordered a few items through the Sears Roebuck Catalog. She was a good cook and knew how to stretch a meal to fill our bellies. We ate mostly what we grew or raised, and the rest came from Mr. Kirkland's store. She was careful with money and kept meticulous records of the monthly spending in a little black notebook. This way of caring for our home and our life brought me comfort. It felt safe and secure, and I knew I was loved.

The fireplace offered comfort to our home, especially when it grew chilly during January and February in Olustee. We didn't have heat or electricity until I was eight so Granny and I appreciated the heat our fireplace provided. However, there was a downside to burning a fire - ashes. Even though the fire was essential to our daily life for warmth, it created a pile of dirty ashes that needed to be cleaned out. If the ashes were not cleaned out regularly, the fire couldn't "breathe" and air would not flow properly to create a good flame needed for heat.

I dreaded cleaning out the dirty ashes. It was a messy, boring job. After waiting for the ashes to cool, I scooped them into a bag or bucket with a small spade. Then I buried them in our backyard by the edge of the woods so wind couldn't stir up soot in the air. Finally I swept the hearth with a small broom. Perhaps doing a job well and participating in the care of our home was one of the ways I comforted Granny. Sitting with her by the clean fireplace in the evenings after the winter sun had set for the day; our bones warmed by the heat, our reading or conversation enhanced by the flickering light, this was indeed shared comfort.

When Granny announced, "Bobby, we're gettin' electricity," one day after I came home from school, I couldn't believe the exciting news. Almost everyone in Olustee had electricity in their homes. The only ones that didn't were rural residents that lived out along the edges of town. There wasn't even a pole to string lines until enough people convinced the Florida Power and Light Company to finally install one. Up until then we used kerosene lamps every evening and pumped our water by hand. The iceman regularly delivered a block of ice for our small ice box and we boiled water on our stove for baths. Electricity changed our lives.

After Granny saved up a little money, we bought an electric water pump that saved us time and energy. Next came a refrigerator to keep our food from spoiling. We could plug in a fan to keep us cool in the sticky Florida heat and a small space heater for the colder months. But the light. The light changed everything. It pushed away the darkness. With one small tug on a string hanging from the ceiling we had instant light. Bright, beautiful, illuminating light! One bulb lit up the room and no matter where you sat you could see well enough to read a book or sew a stitch or see the expression on a face. After a while I couldn't even imagine how we had lived so long without this kind of comfort.

Electricity provided so many modern comforts, but it also charged my thinking with unlimited possibility. Sometimes late at night I lay in bed wondering about all the places I might go, people I might meet, things I might accomplish. The light and power that surged through our home with such ease sparked a restlessness deep inside. I felt something tugging at me. A need to move. To go. To break out of the smallness of my life. I wanted something more. Maybe not at the speed of light, but gradually like a lantern growing brighter little by little.

9
COMMUNITY

"When the roll is called up yonder..."

Each Sunday Granny and I walked to church or rode with Uncle Colonel. Olustee Church of God was a white, clapboard traditional building where twenty to thirty-five of us met each Sunday for worship and fellowship. During Sunday School we pulled curtains across the one-room church to divide open space into rooms. Everyone knew Sunday school was over when we heard the cowbell ring. We pulled the curtains back and Granny and I found our regular spot to sit, the right-hand section, back about four pews, on the end. We settled into those wood-slatted benches and waited for Uncle Colonel to lead the singing. "When the roll is called up yonder...," he'd sing out, pumping his fist in circles close to his chest and completely lost in the moment of worship. Granny and I joined in with gusto even though our voices were not particularly angelic. Sitting on those pews, I belted out all my favorites: "Power in the Blood," "Leaning on the Ever-Lasting Arms," and "I'll Fly Away."

Every few years a new pastor moved into the parsonage and shepherded the congregation. Brother Rich, Brother Agee and my favorite, Sister Ford. Sister Ford preached the Word with enthusiasm and always held a small hanky in her right hand. She was easy to talk to and compassionate. I can still feel her secure, warm hand on my back when she prayed for me at the end of the service sometimes.

I would go up to the altar and receive her prayer for God's blessing on my life. I didn't know exactly what that meant, but I knew her hand on my back was touching a place deep inside me that needed comfort.

I remember one visiting evangelist who scared me spitless. He was a fiery messenger who spoke of awful times "a comin'." Big words like tribulation and condemnation flew out of his mouth like the very flames of hell and when he jumped over the altar and walked through the aisles banging one of the pie tins we used for offering, I paid attention. His voice boomed loud and rhythmic, encouraging people to "get right with God." One evening he painted a terrifying picture of tribulation complete with scorpions coming to sting and bite. Falling asleep was tricky that night. Every little tickle or itch on my legs was a possible scorpion. How was I to know if tribulation was upon me or not? Knowing for sure if you are "right with God" was a bit of a mystery to a ten year old Baker County boy! I prayed all night long.

Sunday night service always had time for testimonies. We waited patiently and eventually different people in the church stood up and shared something about their lives that glorified God. There was an element of excitement waiting to see who would stand up next and wondering what they would say. Except with Granny. Granny always testified, and I knew her testimony by heart because it was the same every time. She'd raise her right hand like she was being sworn in to a court of law and say in one breath, "Not every one that saith unto me, Lord, Lord, shall enter into the kingdom of heaven; but he that doeth the will of my Father which is in heaven." (Matthew 7:21)

Church time was community time. I learned about connecting with God and connecting with people through my church family. Sometimes after church I joined some guys on the small church platform and listened to them pick and strum their guitars. They let me try and even gave me an old guitar to mess with at home. On Friday nights after youth service, I caught lightning bugs outside with my friends while the grown ups chatted about their week. I developed a sense of security outside my home through church. Those early days of my youth and attending church with Granny planted a small, yet mighty seed in my Olustee heart. I could never have guessed the fruitful orchards waiting for me down the road . . . sprung from one, tiny seed.

10
WILLING WORKERS

"Lizzie, do you think we should put in one more row here?"

They called themselves the Willing Workers. Each Tuesday morning Granny and her friends met to quilt and chat. Everyone came to our house, even though it was one of the smaller homes, because Granny had the quilting frame. This contraption was a rectangular shaped frame that hung from hooks in the ceiling of our living room. Granny and the Willing Workers pulled it down with a simple rope and pulley system when it was time to quilt. Getting ready for the Willing Workers actually started the day before with a thorough cleaning. Granny wanted everything spic and span for company. Once everyone arrived, I headed outside to play. The last thing I needed was a roomful of "Grannies" telling me what to do! But sometimes I spied on them from the front porch and listened in on what I considered "boring lady-talk." There was always a little tidbit from their harmless gossip that proved beneficial to me.

A few hours a week in that meager living space, five to six ladies sat and shared their leftover scraps of cloth and gift of craft to piece together quilts for people in need around town or missionaries and people in need around the world. The hope was that the quilts provided some warmth and comfort for lives, cold and forlorn. However, as the Willing Workers knowingly stitched patterns of warmth and comfort into the quilts with their fingers, they unknowingly stitched patterns of encouragement and friendship into their own hearts with their stories. Each of the ladies shared day to day worries and joys while others listened and nodded their heads in agreement or support. Sometimes they shook their heads as if they couldn't believe what they were hearing. Other times they all spoke at once with advice or reassurances. It wasn't unusual for one of the women to tear up while sharing a difficult story. And when they all laughed at once it sounded no different to me than sharp cackling from the old hens roosting in our chicken coop out back.

Granny kept everyone on track with the quilt. She knew how to draw everyone in.

"Annie, your section is looking' real nice."

"Lizzie, do you think we should put in one more row here?"

"Will this color look okay next to this one, Nellie?"

They pieced, puzzled, stitched, and bound. Until after months of Tuesday mornings, a quilt was born. Old, leftover scraps created something new and fresh, warm and comforting.

The last part of the project was the same each time. The ladies would quietly fold the quilt and then each place a hand on it. Someone would pray that the quilt would go to the person or place who needed it most and provide comfort. As the Willing Workers put away their supplies and pulled the quilting frame up to the ceiling until next time, the mood grew slightly somber. The gathering was over for a while. They needed respite for sore fingers and tired eyes. The quilt would leave and find someone in need, but the camaraderie and encouragement pieced and puzzled, stitched and bound into their hearts would stay with them always, a covering of friendship for the weeks ahead.

11
COMPANIONS

"Granny, you know what we need?"

There comes a time in every young boy's life when a special yearning begins. Somewhere between the ages of seven and ten, a boy starts to feel like he's his own person. He makes decisions about what he likes to eat, who he plays with, and how he explores his world, but he still feels restless. Something is missing. Something that comes when called, gives affection with licks to the face, and provides constant companionship. I wanted a puppy and shamelessly badgered Granny about it night and day.

"Granny, you know what we need?"

"What's on your mind, Bobby?"

"We need a dog. A cute little puppy. I can take care of him and you won't have to worry about where I go because I'll always have him with me to keep me safe."

"Bobby, we don't need a dog. They're a nuisance, an extra mouth to feed. Besides, they give you worms!"

Worms were always Granny's concern when it came to dogs. I liked worms and wasn't sure what she had against them, but they were her line drawn in the sand when we had the dog-for-a-pet conversation. Granny was always worried about me getting worms. At some point this conversation played out in front of a certain Uncle who happened to be visiting one Sunday afternoon. He didn't say a word about it, but the next week he showed up with a wiggling puppy in his arms. He gave a vague explanation about how he just found it on the side of the road and thought I would enjoy taking care of it. Granny crossed her arms, pursed her lips, and gave my uncle the stink eye, but all she said was, "The dog stays outside."

I couldn't believe my luck. Finally, after months of begging, plotting, and wishing, I had a real companion. I named the small, black mutt Buddy and loved her fiercely. She slept on the back porch and drank from a little water bowl I put out for her. I fed her leftover scraps from what we ate and played all kinds of games with her. We snuck around underneath the house where it was dark and cool and no one could see us. From between the slats of the front steps we watched the iceman deliver a block of ice or listened to the Watkins Liniment man talk Granny into his lotions, spices, and a special new medicine, Hadacol, evidently the cure to everything. Buddy panted so loudly with her little pink tongue hanging out that I would put my finger to my lips and whisper, "Shhhh." She would whine and lick my face.

We raced around the yard, and I carried her all over town. We walked along the railroad tracks looking for treasures. As much as I tried to keep her away from the chickens, she barked at them every chance she got. Some afternoons we just lay on the back porch together listening to the Yankees on my battery-powered radio. Her favorite thing was to pounce on me and lick my face.

"Worms!" Granny muttered. "That dog is going to give you worms, Bobby!"

Eventually, Buddy had to go back with my Uncle. Even though she never gave me worms, her barking got on Granny's nerves and scared the chickens.

My Uncle Colonel raised cattle and thought since Buddy didn't work out, I might enjoy raising a calf. We paid him $10 for a brown and white calf I named Betsy. Granny tolerated Betsy because she was a farm animal and didn't lick my face. She also didn't bark at the chickens!

I transferred my love for Buddy right over to Betsy. I fed her from a nipple bucket, a contraption most farmers used with their calves. We built her a pen next to the chicken coop and she ate grain out of a little trough. All I had to do was beat my hand against the side of the bucket and Betsy came trotting over lickety-split! She wasn't as entertaining as Buddy and couldn't fit under the house with me, but she liked to take walks around town. I put a rope around her neck and walked her along the same paths Buddy and I walked. One day she managed to run off with the rope trailing behind her like a squiggly snake. I chased her around town all afternoon and finally got her home.

When she had grown enough, Uncle Colonel came and took her back to sell. Buddy was my last pet until much later in life. I reconciled myself to the fact that Granny and pets just weren't compatible. She was much too practical to financially support an animal that didn't contribute to one of the basics for us - food, clothing, or income. Even though Buddy and Betsy didn't stay long, they scratched my itch for companionship. Life was good. But life with a companion was way better.

12
TIES

"I'll remember this day forever!"

There were three small grocery stores in Olustee, but Granny's tab was always at Mr. Kirkland's. From our little house, I could walk up the train tracks and follow them all the way to his store. The tracks were my compass for getting around town. They also provided a sort of playground for my mind because I could walk the tracks without thinking and let my mind weave through the rooms of my imagination. The tracks always led me to my destination. I loved the way the railroad ties followed one right after the other in a pattern that stretched out before me like endless ladder rungs - solid and reliable. If a train was coming you felt the tremor under your bare feet way before you heard the warning bells at the railroad crossings.

My walks along the tracks to Mr. Kirkland's were filled with daydreaming and imagining what my life might become some day. In my imagined future, I was self-sufficient, knowledgeable, rich, and traveling everywhere to play professional baseball, of course. Once I arrived at Mr. Kirkland's I shifted from daydreaming into errand mode and took care of business.

"Good morning, Bobby," Mr. Kirkland greeted me.

"Hi, Mr. Kirkland."

"Shopping' for Granny today?"

"Yes sir."

At this point I handed over the crumpled list from my pocket. Granny always made a list, and the list was usually simple with only the essentials like flour, salt, sugar, coffee, etc.... As I glanced around the store, I saw lots of items I wished were on the list. Sometimes the temptation was just too great.

"I'll take a pack of peanuts and a Pepsi too."

"Are you sure, Bobby? Granny didn't put that on the list?"

Mr. Kirkland always seemed to wear half a smile on his face when he asked me the question.

"That's ok Mr. Kirkland. Just put it on our tab."

Even though it wasn't the craziest thing I ever put on our tab (like the time I ordered a gun C.O.D. from the Sears Roebuck catalog), I knew Granny would find out and scold me later. Still, that didn't subtract one bit from the pure joy a packet of peanuts poured into a cold fizzy Pepsi delivered to my mouth on a hot summer day. Whatever the scolding, it was completely worth it!

It was on one of these walks to Mr. Kirkland's grocery store that something small, yet significant and life changing occurred. As I walked along the tracks a shape on the railroad tie caught my attention. I squatted down to get a closer look and saw a simple triangle etched on the tie. I slowly traced my finger over it repeatedly and stared at it for a long time trying to figure out why it was there and why I noticed it on this particular day. A geometric shape in math was my only knowledge of a triangle. I had no idea it was a symbol for other meanings like the Christian Trinity (Father, Son, Holy Spirit) or the ancient Greek's "doorway to higher wisdom." I only knew that the triangle on the tie stirred a feeling in me. A feeling of hope and desire and determination. A feeling of promise. I would be someone someday. Go places someday. Know where I fit in this world someday. It felt so real and substantial that for a split second this promise filled me up from the soles of my feet to the tips of my ears. It went beyond daydreaming and created a tiny space for my real future to start growing.

"I'll remember this day forever," I whispered to myself. "Forever."

Then I went back to being my nine-year-old self, hopping from one tie to the next all the way to Mr. Kirkland's.

13
RETREAT

"You will come back faster than you go."

The dusty roads I walked in Olustee were made from stories packed down and smoothed out over hundreds of years. Occasionally, I heard old-timers talking about things that had happened a long, long time ago in Olustee. The Battle of Ocean Pond was one such story.

On an ordinary February morning in 1864 General Truman A. Seymour marched Union troops west from the small town of Macclenny in hopes of surprising Confederate troops and occupying enough of Florida to disrupt transportation links and food supplies. The tired, but confident young men were amused by a woman's bold comment to them as they passed by … "You will come back faster than you go." Little did they know how prophetic her words would be.

The confederate soldiers heard about the Union's plan to occupy Florida and secretly prepared for their offense led by Brigadier Generals Joseph Finegan and Alfred Colquitt. Finegan chose the tiny town of Olustee as the best defendable position because of its narrow pass. Ocean Pond, a very large body of water, bordered one side and vast swampland the other. He knew the Union troops would never make it past his men once nature pinned them in on both sides.

Finegan selected groups of soldiers and sent them out to lure the Union troops to Olustee by creating small skirmishes like crumbs leading a mouse to the trap. It worked; and by the time General Seymour realized he and his troops had not only lost the element of surprise, but were being played, it was too late. On a forest floor of virgin pines with no underbrush for cover, the Union fought the Confederates in the only major Civil War battle fought in Florida.

Some call it the Battle of Olustee, some the Battle of Ocean Pond. Mostly, it was a battle of boys and men, fathers and sons, brothers and cousins. It was a battle of blood and sweat and gut-wrenching casualties. In the end, Olustee's narrow pass proved victorious for the Confederates while the Union soldiers retreated back to Jacksonville where they stayed for the remainder of the war.

A different, yet connected story took place on an ordinary afternoon in 1952 when two Olustee boys hopped on their bikes in different parts of town and pedaled down Route 90. One boy was white, the other black. One was riding west, the other east. Neither was paying much attention to anything other than the whistling wind and the sound of spokes spinning faster and faster. When the bikes collided near Walter Davis's store, the boys were more than a little surprised.

I jumped up quickly and brushed the dirt off my clothes. Eyeing the other boy, I looked over my bike to make sure it was okay. He did the same. Neither of us said a word, but we communicated everything with our eyes and a slight nod. Embarrassed and uncomfortable we hopped back on our bikes and pedaled away silently, hoping no one fussed about a white boy and a black boy crashing bikes one afternoon in Olustee.

I'd heard the rumor that a group of white men had tried to kill the black man who was driving the night my parents were killed. The other boy understood justice mostly worked in favor of white families. Even though our bike collision was an accident, and no one was hurt, both of us retreated from any sort of commotion. Almost a hundred years after the Battle of Olustee there were still sides to be on. There was a narrow pass, too narrow even for young boys from opposite sides of town to speak, shake hands, and apologize. But it wasn't Ocean Pond or swamp land that pinned us in; it was dark clouds of prejudice, bitterness, misunderstanding, lies, hate, tradition, and fear. We didn't even know how to name all the things that created too narrow a way for us. We only felt their presence hovering around us, making us feel uncomfortable and a little lost, pinning us in with nowhere to go. It was best to both retreat like nothing ever happened. Maybe someday it would be different.

14
OCEAN POND

"Come on, Bobby," my friends yelled as I took a running
jump off the dock.

It was a broiling, humid July afternoon. The kind that presented only one option for Olustee youth ... Ocean Pond. Ocean Pond was like the community pool; and although it was more the size of a lake than a pond, with all sorts of Floridian creatures calling it home, including alligators, we swam every summer in the cool water. As soon as Granny hesitated for one minute with the next errand or job she had for me, I was on my bike and heading to Ocean Pond as fast as my bare feet could pedal. It didn't matter how hot or tired or frustrated I was, by the time I reached the sandy shore, found my friends, and felt the cool water on my skin, everything else just washed away.

Ocean Pond was an escape from the daily grind. It was a place where a boy could forget about all the things on his mind. He could splash girls and make them squeal, try out new swimming strokes, impress friends with bravery, or shiver with anticipation when an older teen attempted to swim all the way across to the other side. He could jump a little when something brushed against his leg and pray it wasn't one of the alligators everyone talked about, but no one ever saw. Ocean Pond was a summer hangout that still carries a feeling of carefree days and lazy afternoons in my memory.

It was there I learned to swim with uncles and aunts, cousins and friends cheering me on. It was there I mastered diving off the end of the dock where the water was deep and safest. It was there, off Ocean Pond's shore, where Pastor Rich baptized me in the name of the Father, Son, and Holy Spirit in front of my church congregation; the water swallowing me whole and pouring me out as a new creation before all witnesses. I was only eight and didn't fully understand Baptism, but it was a significant spiritual rite of passage for me. One that profoundly illustrates the unconditional love and grace Christ gives despite our lack of fully understanding his Kingdom ways.

I may not have completely understood what I was doing, or more specifically what God was doing in my life, but I did understand being surrounded by friends and family. Wanting to belong. Craving a place I couldn't yet name. I was submerged in lake water, but for the first time, I experienced the power of the Living Water washing me clean from the inside out.

15
DELIVERY

"Listen to the train whistle before you start."

I heard the whistle and felt the vibration of the tracks as I raced across the trestle, hoping to beat the train before it caught up to me. My only other choice was to fling myself over the side and hang on for dear life. This never happened, of course! But it was an adventurous thrill to cross the trestle west of town and shiver with the excitement of knowing it could happen. Every day before I went out to play, Granny's last words of instruction chased after me, "Bobby, you be careful crossing the trestle. Listen for the train whistle before you start."

Trains were a part of everyday life in Olustee back in the 40's and 50's. A passenger train came through town at least twice a day and also delivered mail. Noisy, long, freight trains barreled through day and night exporting pine logs or pulp wood essential to Florida's economy. You had to watch out for the freight trains because they never slowed down or stopped. They just passed through, providing an excellent opportunity for racing on your bike to see how long you could keep up.

The train that held the most excitement for all of us, was the 10 am passenger/mail train. In the morning the train stopped for a while and delivered a large, canvas mail bag at the train depot, a block down from Mr. Kirkland's store. Many of us gathered around the front counter, and watched as Mr. Kirkland retrieved the mail bag. When he returned and disappeared into the back office with the bag, he'd whistle a jaunty tune and get to work. I can still hear the tiny clicking sound the lock made as he opened the bag and began to sort. Then we waited.

Even though the actual mail was typically uninteresting, the possibility of what could be in that mail bag was what drew us all together, waiting in anticipation. Before names were called or mail was doled out, anything could be in that bag. A surprise package or special birthday invitation. A card to make you laugh 'til your belly ached or a letter from a secret admirer to make you swoon. Even the new Sears Roebuck catalog was a fun distraction from the mundane stacks of bills and advertisements. It wasn't just mail, but hope and possibility that the 10 am train delivered to Olustee every morning.

Sometimes Granny received letters from her family. I remember her reading parts of the letters out loud. She skipped other parts that brought a smile or tears to her face and no amount of begging would sway her to read those parts to me. Late afternoon brought one more chance for mail. Mr. Kirkland walked out around 3:45 and hung the bag with the outgoing mail on a post alongside the tracks. At 4:00 sharp, the train passed, but this time it didn't stop. A man leaned out the window with a large hook and grabbed the bag of outgoing mail. If there was any late mail to deliver, he threw it on the dirt road beside the tracks in a small bag that didn't require a lock. Most town folk didn't bother with the 4:00 pm delivery. They just waited until the morning to pick up everything. But for a kid, the afternoon delivery routine was fun to watch.

The possibility of receiving a letter from my dad, Harold Rhoden, always lived in a back corner of my mind. I was hopeful that one of these days he would write to me and tell me all about his time in the war. He would pick a date to come visit and take me out for ice cream or play catch with me. And possibly. Hopefully. I might even show him how to cross the trestle.

16
CHANGES

"Happy Birthday to you..."

The years rolled by for Granny and me. I marked time as most
children do by holidays, birthdays, summer break, and the start of
school. My birthday was in October and Granny's in December so
the autumn months blew by like a freight train barreling through
town with no stops. Holidays anchored the season with birthdays
bobbing in between. Granny usually made vanilla cupcakes with
white icing just the way I liked for my birthday. Mostly it was
a special day because of the sweet treat, but there was always at
least one small package for me to open. It was never anything too
exciting, maybe a new item of clothing I needed; but opening a
package wrapped just for me was still thrilling.

On the first Sunday in December all Granny's children and
their families arrived in the afternoon and held a birthday picnic in
Granny's front yard. Granny was the guest of honor and as people
arrived her front porch grew laden with delicious dishes from
everyone's home. We'd sing Happy Birthday to Granny and then
get down to the business of unsupervised eating. This was always a
festive time with mounds of fried chicken and potato salad, biscuits,
a pot of chicken and dumplings, and garden vegetables. I ate like
there was no tomorrow and washed it all down with sweet tea.
Even with my stomach stuffed to bursting, I always had room for

my favorite dessert: banana pudding. After we ate, the grown ups sat and visited, catching up on all the news and gossip between each other while the young cousins raced around the yard through scrub grass and pine trees to reach a homemade base in a wild game of tag. Occasionally an uncle might join in the game or play catch with us.

During the Christmas season Granny and I found our tree in the woods and cut it down with a small cross-cut saw. It was never majestic or precisely shaped like my aunts' and uncles' Christmas trees, but it added a cozy, festive look to our small home. We used a pot filled with dirt to steady the tree or made a simple stand out of scraps of wood. We strung paper chains and created cut-out angels to hang on the branches. Some years we even splurged for a bit of tinsel and maybe a bulb ornament if we drove into Lake City with Uncle Colonel. Tinsel and a hanging bulb or two created just the right amount of sparkle.

Our tree stood in front of the window in our living room and declared the official arrival of the holiday season at Granny Cobb's. We made or bought each other a small item and wrapped it with old newspaper or brown paper cut from Mr. Kirkland's grocery bags. Green and red crayons marked To: and From: for added Christmas spirit. Even though I didn't really believe in Santa, it was fun to pretend he was bringing all sorts of exciting presents my way. When the relatives came, they carried presents of all shapes and sizes, adorned with ribbons and bows and wrapped in the prettiest holiday gift wrap I'd ever seen. Even though Jacksonville was only an hour's drive from Olustee, it seemed like another world to me. My aunts, uncles, and cousins arrived like the magi, bearing gifts from a foreign land filled with tall buildings, big lights, and department stores. Mysterious, wonderful, abundant Jacksonville.

January through March slowed down with only Valentine's Day to mark the passing time. Olustee grew cooler during these months so we built a fire most days and nights to heat our home until we had electricity. When Spring arrived with promises of balmy, comfortable temperatures, so did Easter and dying Easter eggs. Or rather, coloring eggs with crayons. Granny always made me a new shirt for Easter Sunday, and ordered me a pair of shoes from the Sears Roebuck catalog. Once Easter passed, summer was just around the corner. Summer meant no school, no shoes, fishing, bike-riding, and swimming at Ocean Pond. I never owned a pair of swimming trunks, but cut-off pants worked just fine.

Time flowed in this rhythm for many years. It was a comfortable rhythm that gave me a sense of stability and taught me about how extended families connected and supported each other. I still felt restless and ready for adventure most of the time, but I knew I was loved and cared for and given all the basics I needed in life.

The year I turned twelve was the year of great change. By this time Granny suffered from arthritis and had to move around in a wheel-chair some of the time. I noticed how she needed to rest often and grew more impatient with me by the day. I caught her wiping her eyes one evening while she was standing at the sink. I knew she didn't want me to see her crying, but I didn't know what was making her so sad. Maybe she missed her husband or my mother? Maybe she wished I would help more around the house? Maybe she was just tired and needed a break?

As it turned out probably all those things were true. But the one thing I had no way of knowing, the thing that brought sadness and heaviness to Granny's heart, was realizing it was time. A tired, arthritic woman in her sixties was no match for a strapping, young whippersnapper. It was time for a change. It was time for opportunity. It was time for Jacksonville. Once I understood what was being discussed between Granny and the relatives - my moving to Jacksonville to live with my aunt and uncle and three boy cousins - I couldn't make time speed up fast enough. A big, modern city offered city-sized schools and athletic fields and plenty of activities to keep me busy. My cousins were three more boys to divide the lecture, chores, and nagging. Three more boys to share the fun, trouble, and stories. Three more boys all to myself. Here was my chance to go places, do something, be somebody.

On a balmy Sunday afternoon in December, after celebrating Granny's birthday with the whole family, we packed our Olustee home into the pickup trucks, and drove to Jacksonville. Granny moved in with her daughter, a thirty minute drive from me, and received the care she needed. I moved in with Uncle E.D. and Aunt Inez Dryden and my three cousins or brothers as I grew to think of them. They lived in Wesconnett, the westside of Jacksonville, and I thought their house was the most modern thing I ever laid eyes on with flushing toilets, light switches, a telephone, and a car. Even though I was excited for the change, I missed Granny soon enough and understood why she had been so sad. She understood my excitement for a fresh start and bold adventures, but she also understood that saying hello to a new way meant saying goodbye to an old one.

My old way of life in Olustee lay behind me like a small, well-worn path. Before me stretched a new way, a wide road with bends and curves I couldn't yet see. I embraced this as only a beginning, not fully seeing how it was also an ending. An ending to my childhood. An ending to my small worldview. An ending of the only nuclear family I had ever known.

17
ADJUSTMENTS

"Hurry up! We're gonna be late!"

The excitement of moving is one thing. The work of settling in and adapting to change is altogether different. Every morning at 4919 Wesconnett Boulevard Uncle E.D. woke up early and headed to work at whatever construction site he was running. Aunt Inez helped all of us get out the door to school and maintained the household, school details, and schedules. My cousins Bill, Earl, and Dale knew things about how a five-member family worked that I didn't. For example, they knew to ask their Dad for money, but their mom for permission to do something. They knew how to blame another sibling for something and not get in trouble. Or how much time to spend in the bathroom before someone came banging on the door yelling, "C'mon, open up! I gotta go!" or "Hurry up! We're gonna be late!" I had a lot to learn and fast.

Bill was thirteen and Earl was eleven, so I fit perfectly between them and loved having male companionship. We alternately teased and looked out for Dale the youngest, who was only six. When I moved into the two-bedroom home with the Drydens, I shared a room with Bill and Earl. Dale moved out of the room and onto the living room pull-out couch. Each night Aunt Inez made Dale's bed and in the morning she transformed his bed back into the couch. Even though my moving in created some inconveniences for their family, Aunt Inez and Uncle E.D. welcomed me with open arms and loved me like one of their own sons.

Aunt Inez was a skilled southern cook and provided mouth-watering meals for us to eat around the table. Most evenings we ate a hot meal that rotated between rice with beans and gravy or mashed potatoes and fresh fish we caught. Sometimes we had hamburgers or hotdogs, and her meatloaf was a favorite. But Sunday afternoon lunch was something we loved and anticipated all week long. The dining table groaned under the bounty: platters of fried chicken, bowls of rice and gravy, green beans, homemade biscuits, and a chocolate layer cake with pecans on the top for dessert. My stomach was never fuller than when I lived with the Drydens. It seemed that even with me there, food just multiplied and there was even usually enough for seconds, which felt like heaven to a growing boy.

I was a boy teetering on the precipice of a whole new life, and it was glorious. Between a new school and a new family with siblings, I didn't have a lot of time to miss Granny or Olustee. Sometimes as I lay in bed at night, right before I drifted off to sleep, thoughts of Granny and our rural life in Olustee floated through my mind. But it was more a remembering rather than a longing for. Whenever Granny visited she cried and hugged me tight each time we said good-bye. She loved me so much and hated not taking care of me anymore or seeing me every day. I felt a little guilty that her life was slowing down just as mine was speeding up, but not enough to pine away for something that was over. Most twelve-year-old boys lack the emotional capacity to reflect on things like that for too long. I did wonder about my dad, Harold Rhoden. Now that I wasn't living in Olustee anymore, how would he find me? When I asked Granny about that she said not to worry. I figured she must have sent word to him somehow.

I caught the bus back to Olustee one Saturday shortly after moving to Jacksonville. I wanted to see a girl I liked and say hi to my old friends. She and I sat on her porch swing with our legs dangling over the sides and talked about what it was like for me living in Jacksonville. But after one visit, I left Olustee in the dust. There was no going back for me. Only forward. That's the direction I was headed!

18

CONNECTING

"Stay with it now; you can do it!"

Once I settled into life with the Drydens, I started connecting within Wesconnett. I started a new school immediately; and because it was December, I was the new kid in the middle of the year, which is a hard transition even under ideal circumstances. Not only was the school new, but it was much bigger than my small school in Olustee. I was also considerably younger than all the students in my class because I had skipped second grade and combined 6th and 7th grade into one year. It wasn't necessarily the best decision; but because I was bright and a hard worker, Olustee's small town school system chose to move me along as quickly as possible. Bill and Earl helped educate me on how to handle myself at Lake Shore Junior High with five hundred students. The half mile walk from our house to the bus stop gave them plenty of time to share everything they knew about school in the big city, and I was all ears! Despite my initial excitement though, I realized soon enough that a classroom still felt like a classroom no matter the size.

After school we fished, played "tree tag" hopping from branch to branch in the big oak tree at the center of our neighborhood, found other kids to play a game of touch football, or just biked around. Bill and Earl introduced me to Little League and Pappy Turknet, the iconic Little League baseball coach in the area. I signed up to play on The Bullets, a 10-12 year old summer team, and had the best beginner's luck. Coach made me a starting pitcher and I even pitched one no-hitter. He was a great coach and talked us through the games with encouraging phrases like, "Stay with it now; you can do it!" I surprised myself one game by hitting three home runs. We won the league championship and figured it was only a matter of time before the majors called us up.

I also got a paper route. Unlike some of my other attempts at getting a job in Olustee, my pursuit to make money finally paid off. My short resume included pumping gas for one afternoon at a gas station that wasn't hiring and paid me a dollar just to be nice, working at a logging job for about an hour "dippin" for turpentine until I cut myself on the saw and sat in a hot, pick-up truck all day until someone could drive me home, and a small paper route. With a longer paper route that paid well, I was a working man! I had to be ready by 5:30 a.m. the day the stack of papers was dropped off. Sometimes I arrived too early, but there was a large tree with the perfect boy-sized hole scooped out of the bottom of the trunk where I curled up and napped until the truck arrived. Then I rolled the papers, stretched a rubber band around each one, and placed them in the basket on my bike. While I delivered papers one house at a time, life in Wesconnett delivered a whole new world to me one experience at a time.

Sundays in Wesconnett were different from Olustee. The Drydens didn't attend church like Granny and me, so there was no need for Sunday clothes or getting up early for the service.

At first I didn't mind one bit. Uncle E.D thought most people you met in church only acted like Christians on Sunday and that was too hypocritical for him to stomach. Instead, he chose to worship on the St. John's river fishing for croaker. With a fishing pole in hand rather than the Bible, Uncle E.D. let the chirping birds and croaking frogs preach nature's truth to him. Sometimes I went fishing with him. It was peaceful and gave my mind time to wander. Other Sunday afternoons were spent down at the drugstore playing on the pinball machine or hanging out with friends after stuffing ourselves with Aunt Inez's big Sunday lunch.

I did find my way back to church for a while, although it was in a roundabout way. Linwood Christian Church was located across the street from our house and held dances in the rec hall on Saturday nights. I considered myself a decent dancer and decided I needed to attend these Saturday night dances to meet girls. There was one small problem. The dances were only for church members. Becoming a member of a church for the sole purpose of meeting girls at a dance may seem shallow and adolescent, but I was a 14-year-old adolescent and didn't hold myself to high spiritual standards. Luckily, Uncle E.D. liked the minister at Linwood Christian, and supported my interest in becoming a member.

One of the membership requirements was to be baptized. Even though I had already been baptized in Ocean Pond, I was encouraged to be baptized again at Linwood Christian. I didn't question this. It was another hoop to jump through, not a theological issue to wrestle into submission. The whole Dryden family attended my baptism on a Sunday night at the church and witnessed my becoming a full member. It was nice to have family support. The Saturday night dances were fun and filled me with another sense of belonging. I didn't realize back then that the arm of God is long enough to hold onto a young teen whose fickle heart drags him around on a leash. Even the most fickle heart can sometimes land in a holy place.

19
TROUBLE

"Did you enjoy Kingsley Lake?"

Occasionally attending church and being baptized a second time still didn't keep me out of trouble. When I entered Robert E. Lee High School at the young age of 12, due to skipped grades in Olustee, I struggled with being the youngest in a sea of older, more mature students. I handled the classroom material with no problem, but socially, I had a lot of catching up to do. I was an independent soul, always ready for adventure and excitement; and by senior year I was hanging out with friends who majored in adventure and excitement, with a dash of rebellion.

Before school, we'd meet in the parking lot of Lee's Sandwich Shop where we bought Cuban sandwiches and listened to Jim Lowe sing "Green Door" on the jukebox as we gambled with our lunch money in a game called "match." I also started smoking cigarettes. I remember being hungry many afternoons when I didn't have enough money for lunch because of losing it in a game or buying the Cuban sandwich earlier. Adventure and excitement had a downside.

One day my friends and I decided it was perfect weather for swimming at Kingsley Lake. Unfortunately it was a school day, but we quickly figured out a solution. We ditched school. We thought we were so cool and savvy; however, we were still young teenage boys who only lived for the moment. By the time lunch rolled around, we realized we had no money and were hungry. My cousin, Laverne, lived close by and I was sure she would help us out. She was a young adult and would definitely understand how sometimes you just need a day off school. I convinced my friends to go to Laverne's house; and when we showed up on her front porch saying we were hungry, Laverne invited us in and fed us all the sandwiches our stomachs could handle. Of course as soon as we left, she called Aunt Inez. I imagine the conversation went something like this:

Laverne: "Hi Inez. I thought you should know I just had an interesting hour with Bobby and his friends."

Inez: "Bobby? He's in school."

Laverne: "Well, unless school relocated to Kingsley Lake for the day, no he's not.
He and his buddies just ate an army's worth of sandwiches at my house and smelled like lake water."

Inez: "I see. Thanks for letting me know."

When I arrived home I tried to pull it off like I'd been at school all day. Aunt Inez asked me about school and I was ready with a nonchalant reply about how it was fine and Mrs. So-and-so gave too much homework again. When she raised her eyebrow at me and said nothing, I knew I was busted.

"Did you enjoy Kingsley Lake?"

Before I could even answer, she continued, "I'm not writing you an excuse slip for skipping school, Bobby. You will have to face the consequences yourself."

The truth was even if Laverne hadn't called Aunt Inez, my lobster red face and lake hair would have given me away. I confessed to my homeroom teacher the following day and served my penalty of garden club for three days. Believe me, it was not the kind of club you want to join. To this day, I blame the garden club for my lifelong aversion to yard work!

One of the most memorable days in high school was when I stole a dictionary from Ms. Blackwell's 6th period English Lit. class. No one dared me to do it. I didn't plan on stealing. It just kind of happened. We were working on an assignment in class and using the dictionary. At the end of class, I impulsively slipped it between my other books and walked out. It was so easy I could hardly believe it. We didn't have a dictionary at home and I thought it would be cool to have one. Besides, would anyone even miss it?

The next day Ms. Blackwell announced that the classroom dictionary was missing and did anyone know where it might be? I was on the verge of confessing. It would have been so easy to say, "I'm really sorry. I took it home, but I can bring it back tomorrow." That might have been the end of the conversation with just a mild scolding. But instead I said nothing. I even stayed after and helped her look for it all over the classroom.

"Thanks for all your help today, Bobby," she said as I headed home.

My insides churned with a sick feeling of dishonesty and deceit as I picked at dinner that evening. Later, when everyone was busy, I took the dictionary out of my closet, flopped across my bed, and dropped the hefty book in front of me. Flipping to the front where *Property of Robert E. Lee High School* was stamped in black ink across the page, I moved my hand over those guilt-ridden words. I wished I could just rewind and go back to the day before. I would make a better choice if I could just start over. I knew I should turn it in and tell Ms. Blackwell, but that seemed impossible and too embarrassing. What would she say to me? She would be so disappointed.

Slowly, I drew a line through *Property of Robert E. Lee High School* with a dark pen and closed the book; then with a deep sigh, I hid it under some stuff in the back of my closet and tried to forget about it. As heavy as that dictionary was, it was nothing compared to the guilt that settled in my heart. It spread out, took up space, and surprised me with its weight. Even years later, when I thought it was finally gone, the guilt came back to haunt me.

20
DEPARTING

"There's someone else in this hospital I think you should meet."

While I was growing stronger and more sure of myself, Granny Cobb grew weaker and became completely wheelchair bound from arthritis. Eventually a doctor's visit revealed that her body was also fighting cancer. I was fifteen and a senior in high school when the family admitted Granny to the hospital. No matter how tough and independent you are, nothing prepares you for losing someone you love. Someone who raised and loved you despite hardships. Someone who taught you how to live by a creed of respects, introduced you to God, and gave you a feeling of belonging in this world. Someone who held all that you were and hoped to be deep in her heart. Even though I had pulled away from Granny after the move to Wesconnett, I thought she would always be around. I thought we would have more time. I thought.

As I sat on the edge of Granny's bed and awkwardly held her hand, she grimaced with pain. Part of me wanted to walk out and play pinball at the corner store. Or ride with my friends to the beach and sip a coke, catch a wave. Anything was better than sitting in a hospital room and realizing a person you love is slipping away. Another part of me wanted to keep holding her tissue paper thin hand and never let go. The lump forming in my throat ached and made my sadness feel solid, like something more than just emotion.

Uncle D.C. cleared his throat and motioned for me to follow him as he moved toward the door and into the hallway. Slowly, I moved and joined him. When he put his arm around me, I knew what he was going to say. *Granny isn't getting better. She is going to die soon.* But instead he said, "There's someone else in this hospital I think you should meet." My eyebrows arched and my head tilted to the side. "Who?" I asked. "Harold Rhoden," he replied.

My heart joined the lump in my throat. There was no air to breathe. No words to speak. Just a thickness heavy with questions and uncertainty. I was going to finally meet my father. How was I supposed to greet him? Should I be formal and say sir or Mr. Rhoden? Did he expect me to call him dad? None of these sounded right in my head. Handshake or hug? *How do you do? Nice to meet you? What have you been doing for the last 14 years?* Uncle D.C. smiled, put his arm around me, and said, "Come on. I'll go with you."

Another hospital room. Another edge of the bed. This time I stood tall, wanting to make a good, strong impression. Harold was a large man with wavy, reddish-brown hair. Before I could form a sentence in my head, I stuck my hand out and blurted, "Hi, I'm Bobby." Harold shook my hand and said it was nice to meet me. He made small talk. *"How do you do in school? What do you want to be?"* Then he told me he was married and had four children. "I'll write to you and we'll have you out to the house once I recover," he said.

I'm sure I answered all the questions. Uncle D.C. must have talked too. Everything happened so fast and in slow motion all at once. I left the hospital that day feeling sad and empty that Granny was dying, yet full of wondering about Harold. Had I just started a possible new beginning with my father?

Two weeks later I found myself standing at one last edge, the edge of a freshly dug grave. I watched as they lowered Granny's casket into the ground. She was gone, and I was left to learn how to live in a world without her. I wiped at a tear and blew my nose as an arm hugged my shoulder. It was Uncle D.C. "Bobby, you know you can't bring Granny back." I nodded. "But," he continued, "you can go where she's going." I looked him in the eyes, then looked back at Granny's casket and let out a long breath. I knew what he meant. I had heard about going to heaven for as long as I could remember. My favorite song from church days with Granny was always *I'll Fly Away*. Maybe Uncle D.C. was right. Maybe, just maybe, I could go where she was going. Granny had been on a journey her whole life. A journey to glory. She had finally made it. Her journey was ending while mine was just beginning.

*Granny
Cobb*

*Martha Lee Cobb,
Bob's biological mother*

Drew Strickland, Bob's biological father

Martha Lee and Harold Rhoden who married to give Bob a name

Martha Lee and Ashley Weeks, both died when Bob was two

Little town where Bob grew up

"PU" house

Bob at Ocean Pond

TO

21
WILD

"This one's done, boys. Put the flag on it and let's call it a day."

Mr. Sadler, our boss, leaned against the green work jeep with a look of satisfaction and watched me and my coworkers, Jim and Johnny, finish pounding in the last stake on this project. With his white moustache and cowboy hat, Mr. Sadler could have passed for an authentic cowhand any day of the week. It was September 1958 and I was working in West Palm Beach, Florida for Rubin Construction, a company with a Civil Engineering Department.

After graduating from high school in June, Uncle E.D.accepted a new job and moved the family to Lantana, a small town just south of West Palm Beach. Since I was only 15 and had no solid plans for the future, I moved with them and got my first full time job with Rubin Construction Company thanks to some connections from my Uncle. I made a dollar an hour which was minimum wage back then and figured if I worked hard enough, I could afford some of the nicer things in life. Besides, I was good with numbers and measurements and thought I might study to be an engineer. I registered myself to start classes in January at Palm Beach Junior College and focused on making and saving as much money as possible until then. Living near Palm Beach with its vacation homes, upscale shops, and restaurants made my mouth water for affluence. A list of all I could buy with my savings began to form in my head and at the very top of that list was a car. In a month I would turn 16 and couldn't wait to get my drivers' license.

The job with Rubin involved measuring out plots of land that had once been wild, but were now being cleared for development. Each morning Jim, Johnny, and I drove out in the green jeep and because I was lowest in rank, I rode in the backseat with all the equipment we needed for the project. We chatted and joked with each other. Fresh. Strong. Ready for the day.

We measured distances with a long metal chain on a wheel, drove wooden stakes in the dry dirt with a sledgehammer to mark measurements, and attached a red flag to the top of each stake clearly indicating its position. Most of the time we staked out plots of land for parking lots since Rubin Construction was primarily a paving company. Occasionally, we mapped out roads and pothole locations so the asphalt workers knew exactly where to repair the broken places. The work was tedious and the sun scorched our skin, but the days' end brought a sense of accomplishment as we viewed the surveyed land and knew that someone, somewhere would benefit from this precise boundary we measured. The land had a future.

At dusk we packed the equipment in the jeep and drove back to Rubin's storage building. The ride was quiet as the day's work settled in our bones. Sweaty. Weary. Ready for rest. On those warm West Palm Beach evenings in the back of the jeep my mind wondered about all sorts of things. What lay ahead for me? How would it feel to take college classes? Where would I end up? When would Harold, my father, invite me to meet his family? Could Granny still see me and was she still proud of me? How did God really fit into all of this? My future felt uncertain, unknown, even a little scary.

I didn't realize it at the time, but my wondering mirrored some of the physical labor I was doing every day; each question, a sort of plotting and measuring about the way I pictured my future. Could people be developed like the land? Could a person map out precise boundaries and stake a future for themselves? What about the broken places in a person? Could those be repaired?

I hoped so. I hoped so with all my heart which felt like an expansive, wild piece of land just waiting to be developed.

22
HOPE

"Can I help you with something, son?"

The man's kind face peered in at me through the passenger window I had rolled down. It was a mid-October Sunday morning with a slight coolness in the air that suggested the brutal summer heat was finally moving on. I woke early and felt a strong desire to go to church. Maybe I felt guilty about drinking and smoking at parties? Maybe I felt a little lost and was curious to revisit the faith of my childhood? Maybe I just missed Granny and wanted to feel close to her? The Holy Spirit has a way of nudging us and can use our emotions to lead us in the right direction. All I know is that I woke up with an unexplainable yearning for God.

I remembered seeing a small church nestled behind a drugstore up the road from our house. So I asked to borrow Uncle E.D.'s car and headed out to find God. However, when I pulled in past the sign reading "Lantana Community Church" and parked, I was puzzled to find the small parking lot empty and the church doors locked. Why would a church be locked on a Sunday morning? I jumped back in the car and pulled out slowly, wondering what to do, when I noticed a man walking along the side of the road. He was dressed nicely and looked to me as if he might be walking to church. I pulled over and rolled down the passenger window. The man stopped walking and bent over to look inside the window.

"Can I help you with something son?"

"Excuse me, sir. I was trying to go to church this morning, but the doors are locked and it doesn't seem like anyone's there. Do you know anything about that church?" I asked and pointed behind me.

He grinned. "You're in luck. Today is the first Sunday in our new building. I'm headed there right now"

I grinned back, "Hop in and I'll give you a ride."

I sat through the service and recognized some of the songs from when Granny and I attended church. After the service, a lady named Audrey Davis came up and introduced herself to me. She was so friendly and engaging that I immediately felt comfortable with her and began to talk a little bit too. She introduced me to her husband, Paul, and their six year old son, Greg.

Audrey and her husband, Paul, were lay leaders that helped with the youth at Lantana Community Church, and Paul also led worship on Sunday mornings. They spent time with me, asking me questions about myself and why I decided to visit the church. Both of them were so interesting and genuine; I had never been around Christians with this kind of affluence and intelligence. They encouraged me to come back the next week. I drove home with a contentment I hadn't felt in a long time. Belonging. Community. Possibility. At the young age of 16, I couldn't name exactly what I felt, but I knew I wanted to go back for more. Besides, there was a cute girl in the choir I wouldn't mind seeing again.

Over the next few weeks, I attended Lantana Community Church and sensed something begin to take shape in me. It wasn't until listening to a guest speaker, Dr. Woodhouse, preach one evening during revival week at church that I knew I needed to make a decision. Was I going to follow Christ and serve Him with my whole life or not? There was a pull on my heart I couldn't ignore. I wanted more. More than nostalgia. More than doing the right thing. More than rubbing shoulders with impressive, smart people and feeling a part of something. I didn't want just Sunday Jesus; I wanted everyday Jesus. I prayed that night for him to be everything in my life. I asked him to forgive me for being a sinful person. I invited him not only to help me live my life, but to lead my life.

And just like that, even though nothing changed ... everything changed. I wasn't sure how I was going to explain the change in me to friends and family or if they would even notice. All I knew was that instead of always hoping my life would amount to something, I could now trust in the hope I'd been given. I didn't need to hope. Christ was my hope. He was the good news I didn't even know I wanted to hear. I rolled down the window on the drive home and let the night autumn air in. It was a beautiful night, but it wasn't just any night. It was the night hope became a noun.

23
CALLED

"Come in, Bob."

I walked into the classroom nervously and sat down in front of Mr. Wyatt's desk. My hands clenched the graded math test, worn from so much rolling and unrolling. My first "F" felt personal and discouraging. More than a simple statement on my mastery of content, it felt like a statement on what my future might look like. I had always excelled in math, so naturally, when I enrolled in Palm Beach Junior College to study engineering, I felt confident in my ability to do well. I was rattled and needed to talk to Mr. Wyatt.

Besides working for Rubin Construction, I became more involved with Lantana Community Church. My relationship with Jesus grew and the Davis family nurtured me in a way that brought to mind Granny Cobb's fierce love for me and her absolute faith that God was in control. Over meals around their table and conversations about God's plan for me and how the gifts he had given me could be used, my physical and mental needs were nourished. Through Bible studies and youth group my spiritual and emotional needs were not just nourished, but lavished with love, acceptance, and a new sense of direction.

I had no idea how thirsty I was for relationship. Paul Davis became a strong father figure in my life and encouraged me to grow close to my heavenly Father as well. Harold Rhoden hadn't been available, but suddenly I had an abundance of "fathering." Where once I had been empty and void, I was now downright saturated. I was starstruck, following the *Son* who gave me worth and saw me as worthwhile all in one massive act of love.

Paul and Audrey were smart, creative people who enjoyed working with youth. They were easy to talk to and created an atmosphere of acceptance, belonging, and purpose. One of everyone's favorite youth group activities was "red tie night." Whenever Paul showed up to church on Sunday wearing a red tie, everyone knew something fun was going to happen after youth group Sunday night. It might mean going out for pizza, ice cream, or playing games at someone's house. Even though the concept was simple, it generated a lot of enthusiasm and had us all watching Paul's ties each Sunday!

When Paul and Audrey asked me if I would help serve in the youth group as a student leader I agreed and was proud to be asked, but wasn't exactly sure what a student leader did. They asked me to share my story one night. It was the first time I had ever stood in front of a group of people to speak about something personal. Afterward, several teens came up to me and said how much they liked my talk. Paul and Audrey praised my speaking skills and said they thought I had a gift for communicating. They wondered if I had ever considered going into ministry and told me about a Bible College in Georgia they thought would be a great place for me to study. I agreed to pray about it. I had never thought about working in the ministry and was curious. Did I have leadership skills? Was I a good speaker? Was God somehow calling me to change my course, which had barely started, and go to bible college?

My days continued in a predictable routine. I worked, attended classes, completed assignments, helped out at church, and prayed that all of this would provide a clear vision for what came next in my life. I had a serious girlfriend, Sarah. She and I spent lots of time together talking and transforming her living room into a dance floor many Saturday nights. I even thought she might be the one I would marry someday. No one in my family had ever attended school past high school, so I didn't have strong examples of pursuing further education. No one in my family had ever studied to go into the ministry, so I didn't have the legacy of a long line of preachers to follow; but Granny had always prayed about everything. Her example came back to me and I knew that with Christ as my hope, my future would come together. So I prayed and waited.

When I got my first college math test back and saw the "F", I was devastated and confused. School had always been so easy. I was embarrassed to meet with Mr. Wyatt, but knew I had to talk with him. Maybe he could help me decide if college was right for me. Mr. Wyatt had never taught a student as young as me in college and listened patiently while I told him about Lantana Community Church and the Davises. He nodded as I explained about wrestling with the idea of studying to become a minister and attending Bible College or continuing with my studies in engineering. When I was done, I felt a little silly. Why was I telling my math professor all this?

"Bob, I think going to Bible college and studying to become a minister could be very satisfying for you. Sometimes people see things in us that we can't see in ourselves."

Mr. Wyatt's response surprised me. I knew he was invested in teaching students about math, but apparently he was also invested in teaching students about life.

"Now, about this math test."

Mr. Wyatt told me I had the ability to complete the math course and encouraged me not to let one failing grade stop me. His kind words motivated me and I passed every test after that and finished the course with flying colors. More importantly, something else was developing inside me. The Davises and Mr. Wyatt both used encouragement as boundary markers in my life and helped me see a new direction I could go. Like wild land that is excavated, moved around, filled in, and settled - my heart too, began to settle.

24
POTENTIAL

"Does this look right?"

I stared back at my image in the mirror while Marvin, my roommate, peered over my shoulder with a smirk on his face. He reached over and with one effortless tweak, both tightened and centered the knot in my new tie.

"That's it. You got it!" he crooned and slapped me on the back.

Learning to tie a half-windsor knot was one of a thousand new experiences I encountered my freshman year at Toccoa Falls Bible College. The school was in Toccoa, Georgia, a small town nestled at the foothills of the Blue Ridge Mountains. Before I left, neighbors in Lantana gave me a used suit coat and tie for Toccoa's required Sunday dress code. I had never owned anything so formal and was extremely grateful to these friends.

After many nights of praying, hours of talking with the Davises, a nod of approval from my aunt and uncle, and support from Lantana friends and neighbors, I packed up my less than reliable light green '53 Ford Mainline in late August of '59 and crossed over the Florida-Georgia line to start my new life. I was only sixteen, but had waited my whole life to go somewhere. Do something. Be somebody. I was excited and ready to change the world, but there was a poignant sadness in leaving all I had ever known and loved. The biggest comfort was knowing that Christ, my hope, traveled with me. He was my new home and the feeling of belonging to him, of experiencing his presence no matter where I went, was as reassuring as a slice of Granny's warm custard pie.

I completed one semester at Palm Beach Junior College and saved the rest of my earnings for first semester's tuition at Toccoa. I also received a pension once a month from the government that helped. Months before my mother and her new husband, Ashley, were tragically killed, Ashley had registered papers to adopt me. Because of his service in the navy and the completed adoption paperwork, I was granted financial aid after his death. This extra money helped Granny raise me, and then supplied my aunt and uncle with some extra income when they took me in at the age of 12. Now the monthly checks could help pay for my college tuition.

Funny how one small decision, one signed document, could generate so much provision and future. In almost every way, Ashley Weeks had been more present for me in his death, than Harold Rhoden ever was in his life. After our brief meeting in the hospital, I never heard from Harold again. There was no phone call. No letter. No visit to his farm. Harold Rhoden was my father in name only and I made peace with that. It seemed that my physical and spiritual life stories were running parallel. Most of my life, it turned out, had already been paid for in checks, by my adoptive father, Ashley Weeks. All of my life had most certainly been paid for in love by my heavenly Father who adopted me as his own and purchased me with incredible sacrifice.

Supporting myself through college meant working a job or two along with attending classes. Before working at Rubin Construction, I ran paper routes, bagged groceries at Winn Dixie, cleaned a shoe store every night after closing, and helped deliver furniture for a local store as needed. I couldn't remember a time growing up when I was not on the lookout for an opportunity to make a few dollars. Toccoa's work policy required all freshman and sophomore students to work a job on campus. The pay was credited toward your tuition account. One of my first jobs on campus was a 3 hour shift at the power plant which provided electricity for the campus using water that flowed down from the lake. I worked from 4-7 am each morning and regulated the valve to allow more water through when needed. The force of the water turned the generator and provided electricity for the whole campus. Sometimes, I napped and was late adjusting the valve for the students and faculty who were stirring. Students who knew I worked the early morning shift would chide me and say, "Bob was sleeping on the job this morning."

Piece by piece, like a beautiful quilt made by Granny's willing workers, this is how I came to trust in God's provision for my life. All four of my Toccoa years were stitched together with monthly pensions, hard work, clothing donations, prayer from loved ones, and encouragement from mentors. I grew into a young adult at Toccoa. I made new friends, met new challenges, embraced new ideas. The campus motto was printed on a sign over LeTourneau Hall: *Where Character is Developed with Intellect*. These words lived out by my professors helped shape my thoughts and actions. Ministry tracks were carefully placed in my life through classes, chapels, and special seminars. I matured academically, emotionally, and spiritually.

One afternoon my speech professor, Ms. Unruh, asked me to consider reading for the lead in the school play, "A Man Called Peter." Peter Marshall, the main character, was a minister and I was studying to go into the ministry, so it seemed as good a qualification as any. I agreed to read for the part, even though I had never spoken on a stage in front of a large crowd before nor been interested in dramatic productions. Ms. Unruh was young and attractive, and I doubt any male student at Toccoa would have said "no," to her. Surprisingly, I landed the lead and my quick memory helped with remembering the lines. After months of practice under Ms. Unruh's direction, we put on the production.

I definitely had opening night jitters, but I played the part of Peter Marshall in front of hundreds of people and was shocked by how acting energized me. The stage transformed me from a little Baker County boy to a stately, wise and ministerial young man. Even though I only played the character, I carried something of Peter Marshall around with me after that. I felt changed. Apparently, I had God-given gifts and public speaking was one of them. Somehow, when I spoke in front of all those people, I felt confident in who I was. Ms. Unruh saw something in me; she saw potential leadership and public speaking skills that held the power to influence others. More importantly, Ms. Unruh encouraged me to explore this gift. She, like Mr. Wyatt and the Davises, was another boundary setter helping develop the wildest parts of me into the man God was calling me to be.

25
UPS AND DOWNS

"Joy to the world, the Lord is come."

I was driving back home for the holidays listening to Bing Crosby on the radio and crossing my fingers that the 'ole 53 Ford would make it to Lantana without breaking down.

My Uncle and Aunt had moved from Lantana back to Wesconnett during my freshman year at Toccoa, but I really wanted to see my old church friends, especially the Davises. I needed to spend time with people who understood what my life was like now at Toccoa Falls Bible College. Uncle E.D. and Aunt Inez approved as long as I had a place to stay and a way to get there. Another student at Toccoa who was from Lantana Community Church invited me to stay with him over Christmas break. I agreed and was excited to see everyone again, but it proved to be a difficult holiday.

My relationship with Sarah ended, and my host was not the best influence. He attended Toccoa because his parents thought it would help change his life, but his heart wasn't in it. I underestimated the power of a friend's influence combined with loneliness, and ended up returning to some unhealthy habits over the holidays that were not good for me or my relationship with God. I even started doubting if I really wanted to go into ministry. I knew a pastor's income would never amount to much. Maybe I should focus on making money so I could finally have the nice things I dreamed about!

Visiting with the Davises and talking about college was the highlight. I loved them like family. They could see I was struggling and invited me to stay with them whenever I was in town after that. They also encouraged me to pray about my concerns and at least finish out the school year. I returned to Toccoa for my second semester confused and frustrated. My car was constantly breaking down and I never knew if I was going to have enough money to get through the year. Once again I underestimated the power of influence, but this time it came from students and professors who were like-minded in Christ and believed in the power of a call to ministry. Professors like Ms. Unruh challenged me and restored my belief in God's plan for me. I began to feel that pull again; the Holy Spirit tugged on my heart and nudged me back in the right direction.

We had to pick a weekly service team to join so I chose the Stephens County Jail. Playing the part of Peter Marshall on stage gave me the confidence I needed to preach my first sermon. I preached up a storm in that county jail. I paced and inflected my voice and gave it all I had on Namaan dipping in the Jordan river and being healed. The inmates were of course a captive audience, but they listened and some even asked for prayer at the end. I floated home knowing I had found my calling.

Over spring break I returned to Jacksonville to visit Aunt Inez and Uncle E.D. It was good to see them and my cousins. I enjoyed home-cooked meals and catching up on sleep, but there was one particular unfinished piece of business I came back to face. During Toccoa's spiritual emphasis week I heard a speaker who really challenged me. He spoke on making things right with God, even the small wrongs that seemed insignificant. He spoke on being used by God and encouraged all of us to right the wrongs in our life that might keep us from moving forward in Christ. The stolen dictionary from my high school days traveled with me to Toccoa. Every time

I used it I saw the crossed out words stamped on the inside page, *Property of Robert E. Lee High School.* I stole the dictionary a long time ago before I knew Christ personally, but it still nagged at me.

I don't remember all the details of walking into room 106 at Robert E. Lee High School, returning the stolen dictionary to Ms. Blackwell, or apologizing. However, her response and how she made me feel is still crystal clear and became a watershed moment for me on the power of grace and forgiveness. She hugged me with both arms and said, "Bobby, I think you're going to make a wonderful minister someday."

I walked out of her room unjudged, redeemed, and forgiven. Sure of God's calling on my life. Sure of God's hand in our lives. Sure of God's mission to redeem this whole broken world. Someday.

26
CONNECTIONS

"Bring me something good today, Bob."

I grinned as I drove off in my new 1960 Falcon. It was light blue with four doors and absolutely no mechanical issues, unlike my '53 Ford. After navigating the world of auto repairs for months with my old Ford, I finally had enough savings to pay a monthly car bill. I had worked hard all summer back in Jacksonville loading trucks for an auto warehouse. It was hot, difficult work for a tough boss who made it his mission to tease me about being a "preacher boy" every chance he got; but by the middle of August I had enough money saved to trade in my Ford for a new Falcon and still make first semester tuition. I was too young to sign the papers myself, so my aunt and uncle graciously signed for me to buy the new car.

I was back for sophomore year and enjoying one of my newly appointed positions on campus, "the mail guy." Each day someone had to pick up the college mail in town at the local Post Office. Since I now had a reliable car and was willing to do any odd job, I was the perfect guy for this errand. I remembered watching Mr. Kirkland with the mail bag in Olustee and waiting for the mail as a young boy. Now I was handing out the mail! It didn't hurt that there was a small stipend and a lot of positive attention from the student body whenever I delivered letters from lovers, envelopes with money, and packages of mom's baked goods. "Bring me something good today, Bob!" they would call out after me. Everyone loved "the mail guy."

I also worked in the school print shop and acted as associate editor of our yearbook. I was in charge of selling ads to businesses in town and because I was persuasive, I sold lots of ads. I even used my newly discovered leadership skills to recruit a team to help me. Invitations to speak at local churches on Sundays started rolling in too. Particularly Sundays that were focused on youth. My friends began to recommend me to their pastors and I developed a reputation for being a gifted speaker to youth.

If Freshman year was a rollercoaster of ups and downs, sophomore year was the smooth glide of a boat over water like glass. One positive experience after another seemed to fall in my lap. I was starting to gain wisdom and confidence by learning from my mistakes. I made better decisions, sifted through friendships that had a negative impact on my life, accepted forgiveness, and started trusting the still, small voice of God I began to recognize.

At the end of the school year I decided to live with Paul and Audrey Davis for the summer and work for Rubin Construction again. The Davises were now attending Bethel Assembly of God in Lake Worth and invited me to go with them while I was in town. Apparently, they had told the pastor and some others all about me. They introduced me to John Wilkerson, the pastor, and I knew immediately that I wanted to study everything about him. He was young, but married and had two children. He played the guitar and sang. He loved people and people loved him. When he led worship he had a unique presence that connected with people even from the pulpit. He was everything I hoped to be once I entered the ministry. John took me under his wing for the summer and mentored me. He let me tag along and observe in meetings; we spent time talking about ministry and my future. Many of these conversations were over lunches in restaurants, and he paid for all of it! He also introduced me to his brother-in-law, Ira Stanphill, a well-known

Christian song writer. Ira had founded the church, but only stayed a few years before turning it over to John.

Ira took an interest in me as well and treated me one night to a glorious steak dinner at a fancy restaurant. For a poor college student, this was a small slice of heaven. While we ate, he told me his story which was sad and full of tragedies like my own. He shared that some of the best songs he ever wrote came out of that pain. I was mesmerized by his story and felt a kinship to him. I had never met anyone with a story like mine and certainly never heard anyone talk about beauty coming from pain like that. When we left the restaurant, Ira handed me a $20 bill and said, "Bob, follow God, no matter what happens." I stood there speechless and in awe. How could someone I barely know affect me like that?

I experienced the Holy Spirit in a very unique way that summer. At Bethel they called it being baptized in the Holy Spirit. While I was praying an overwhelming feeling washed over me and caused me to speak in a heavenly language called glossolalia. I didn't completely understand it, but I couldn't deny it based on my personal experience. I felt a deep closeness with God whenever it happened. By the end of the summer John Wilkerson told me he thought I had special gifts for working with youth and suggested I intern at his church the following summer after my junior year. He also planned to tell his nephew, David Wilkerson, who led Teen Challenge, a new ministry to youth in gangs and drug addicts in New York City. John thought David might want me to come to NYC for part of the summer as well and work with him. I knew of David Wilkerson mostly because of his new book that had recently been published, *The Cross and the Switchblade*. He started and ran a groundbreaking ministry on the streets of New York City and I was being recommended to join him? I just kept nodding while John Wilkerson spoke. This was incredible.

I returned to Toccoa for my junior year with confidence and experience. I was Editor of the yearbook, for a stipend of course, and vice president of the student body. I felt much more confident about my calling to the ministry and figured the serious ministers always went to the mission field. So it was settled, I was going to be a missionary somewhere. James Lindsey, known as "Pop" Lindsey, was my Psychology and General Theology professor. He had a dry sense of humor and a master's degree from Wheaton College. The book *"Through Gates of Splendor,"* had a profound impact on me that year. It was the true story of five missionaries who were martyred in the mountains of Ecuador. Most of them were alumni of Wheaton College. I wondered if I could ever get a master's degree from a place like Wheaton College. With all the twists and turns my life had taken, anything seemed possible.

By the time summer rolled around again, everything was set for me to intern at Bethel and work with Dave Wilkerson and Teen Challenge in NYC. I returned to Lake Worth for June, then spent the month of July interning in New York. Even though New York wasn't another country, I was pretty sure gang members and drug addicts counted as a mission field. God and I were going to march in there and take that city by storm. I was 19 and full of vim and vigor. The gangs would disperse. Drug addicts would weep out of repentance and be delivered from addiction. Weapons would be rendered useless. I had no idea how much I was going to learn.

27
POWER

"There is power, power, wonder-working power in the blood of the lamb..."

Walking briskly past the tough-looking group of young men, I sang loud and off-key as confidently as I could. It was well past midnight in a rough section of Brooklyn, and I was both relieved and terrified to recognize my surroundings. I was within a few blocks of my "home" for the summer, but I was alone and out in the streets when I should have been asleep in my bed.

Earlier that evening, I had gone out with friends to evangelize the streets of New York. At some point we split up and I took a subway back to Clinton Avenue where I was staying for the month of July as an intern with Teen Challenge. Apparently I hadn't mastered the subway lines as well as I thought. After hours of riding the train and repeatedly getting lost, I finally recognized a stop and got off. Walking alone at this hour in a neighborhood charged with gang rivalry and racial tension was not my best idea, but I had to get home. I was young, naive, and a prime target if anyone wanted to give me a hard time. Clinton Avenue was just a few blocks down and unfortunately, the only way to get there was walking past this intimidating bunch of guys. I didn't have a zip gun or a switchblade or a swinging chain to protect myself; but I did have my voice and the power of Christ. These would have to do.

I took a deep breath and started singing boisterously. The guys stared me down as I walked by them, but I looked straight ahead and hoped they couldn't see my heart beating through my chest. I noticed one young man out of the corner of my eye making the "crazy" sign to his friends with a finger circling in front of his ear. That was fine with me. Crazy was better than dead. Once I rounded the corner I took off running just in case they changed their minds. I was never so happy to walk through the front door of 416 Clinton Avenue and slip into my bed in the dorm room I shared with some other guys.

New York City was a fascinating place. People lived all kinds of lives - the good and the bad, the sweet and the savory, all mixed up together like one big pot of stew. Lights were on somewhere all night. It didn't matter what time it was day or night, there was always a restaurant open and ready to slap a greasy plate of food down on the table. Tad's Steakhouse was a favorite for me and my friends. For $1.25 you could get a steak, baked potato, and salad. To a small town, country boy, this city felt exciting and adventurous. My mind pulsed with new ideas and my body with endless energy. I wanted to practice all I had learned in the classrooms at Toccoa, and David Wilkerson was more than happy to let me.

Teen Challenge had grown quickly over 3 years and the need was so desperate David couldn't keep up and relied heavily on volunteers. In those days there were no permission slips needed for young, eager Christian youth to help spread God's word to the down and out. Danger was only a problem if you left without your Bible and didn't call on the power of Jesus Christ hourly. Every morning the staff held chapel. We prayed earnestly for people we didn't know yet. We begged God for guidance. We pleaded with him for courage. We stormed the gates of Heaven for hearts to change. Some evenings we went to Spanish Harlem and helped with street services led by Nicky Cruz, a former gang leader who had accepted Christ as his Savior and was leading a whole new gang now for Christ.

On Friday and Saturday nights I preached from a tiny storefront we called Coney Island Chapel, located on the infamous Coney Island. My heart raced and adrenaline pumped through me as I told others about Christ's sacrifice for us and how he could change their lives. After awhile I got pretty good at inflecting my voice like a bonafide evangelist. My friends joked that I was the "Billy Graham" of Coney Island, and I didn't mind the comparison. I knew something else though. More than the rush of adrenaline. More than the attention of a hushed crowd. Even more than the ability to deliver a mini sermon in rhythmic cadence with polished vocabulary, was the power of the Holy Spirit pouring into me while I was preaching. It was like I was being filled with God's presence and then the very power of the presence flowed right out of me to others, yet never left me empty. I was a conduit, a vessel, a channel. That summer I saw the results of a living, breathing faith and all it required was to go boldly and tell everyone the good news. I wonder now sometimes, if maybe we've traded in that zealous, bold faith for one that's safer or more controlled.

One evening as I was preaching at Coney Island Chapel some young men walked by, stuck their heads in and pointed at me. "We're coming after you, preacher," one of them sneered. Before I could even think it through, I flung my arm around like I was pitching a fastball, pointed a finger at them, and yelled in a loud voice, "If you don't repent of your sins you will die and go to hell!" They took off running and I resumed preaching. I guess you could say all those years of practicing my pitching stance, and that one afternoon of pitching rotten eggs at Granny's old smoke house strangely prepared me for God's work.

28
FAVOR

"Wake up, Bennie! The donuts are going to be overcooked."

Mr. Williford must have said this once a week to Bennie, the guy who fried all the pies made in Mr. Williford's bakery. The pies were made in the early morning hours and we were all sleep deprived. But Bennie? Bennie was a legend. He could actually sleep standing up while holding the basket of pies in the deep frier.

I returned for my senior year at Toccoa after a life-changing summer in New York. No one deserves God's favor, but we all experience it in different seasons of our life. My senior year felt like the year of God's favor. When I left Teen Challenge at the end of July, David Wilkerson offered me a job after I graduated. I couldn't say yes fast enough, and he promised to contact me in the coming spring.

I landed a job working in Mr. Williford's bakery from 1 to 6 am every morning Monday through Friday and made $30.00 a week, which was a coveted paycheck in those days. My job was to roll out the dough and make small fruit pies for Bennie to fry. Mr. Williford was the only one in charge of donuts and had the special touch in making the dough and rolling it out.We could eat as much as we wanted, and for a while I thought I would never tire of those sweet treats. Eventually though, I wondered if I would ever be able to stomach another fried pie or donut as long as I lived. I also wondered if I would ever enjoy a full night of sleep again. There were many mornings when I arrived back at the dorm to get ready for class and was so tired I could not remember driving back from the bakery.

I became President of the Ministerial Association which involved directing all the Christian Service activities for the students. My classmates elected me, but they also pressured me as a leader. It turned out to be excellent preparation for some of the hurdles I would face in pastoral ministry years later. Also, my Teen Challenge summer experience opened many new doors of ministry for me. I was invited to a friend's church in Alabama to lead a weekend youth outreach. I had developed a new sermon over the summer titled, "The Downlook, Inlook, Uplook, and Outlook." I tried this out in as many churches as I could my senior year. People, especially youth, responded. Invitations to speak at other churches and youth retreats on the weekends started rolling in. I was barely 20 and feeling like I had the world by the tail. If only Granny could see me now. I knew this was God's work and practiced humility as much as a 20 year old can, but having a gift and being sought after were new developments in my life. I navigated the best I could.

By my last semester at Toccoa, I had fallen behind in tuition payments. Even though I was always working and took extra speaking engagements, I kept coming up short. The finance department knew my situation and that I was paying my way through with little to no family support. They extended a lot of grace over the years, but I was still about $800.00 short and graduation was around the corner. I knew if I couldn't settle my tuition bill, I couldn't graduate. After sharing this concern with Aunt Inez one evening while visiting over a break, I learned that Granny had purchased some U.S. government bonds for me back during the Olustee years. Maybe it was time to cash those in? Aunt Inez and Toccoa's business manager encouraged me to go to the federal office in Atlanta and present the bonds. It turned out that the bonds had matured and the cash amount was $800.00 exactly. Once again, God provided for me in a creative way. I paid off my tuition and prepared to graduate.

I waited anxiously for David Wilkerson to finalize my ministry opportunity with him. What if he forgot about me? What would I do if he never called?

"Bob, meet me in Atlanta next week," Dave said over the phone one evening in April.

He told me he was speaking and wanted me to come to the service. Afterward we would work out the details for me to join the staff at Teen Challenge. I hung up the phone and breathed easily for the first time in a few months.

The church in Atlanta was packed. Dave was becoming a popular speaker at youth gatherings around the country because of his book, *The Cross and the Switchblade,* and his excellent communication skills. He was ahead of his time in describing his ministry to drug addicts and gang members in New York City. Young people were captivated by his bold preaching style; I admired his passion and was in awe of him. Dave shared with me that he wanted me to spend a few weeks in New York after graduation and then become a traveling evangelist for Teen Challenge to raise money for a rehabilitation farm he had built in Rehrersburg, Pennsylvania. When Dave Wilkerson introduced me at the youth rally as someone who would be joining him to work at Teen Challenge in June, my status rose instantly with my peers. I was on top of the world. Stakes were in the ground. Boundaries plotted out. Wild land developed.

29
GOD'S MOUNTAIN

"I'll preach and focus on bringing people to Christ.
God will take care of the money."

It was June of '63 and I remember saying those words to Frank Reynolds like it was yesterday. I had graduated from Toccoa, packed my belongings, enjoyed some time with my aunts and uncles before hugging them goodbye, and headed straight to NYC. I didn't know when I would be back. I didn't know where I was going to end up. I didn't even know how someone like me who ran to school barefoot and watched trains pass through town for fun could now drive across several state lines in my own car to work with a man like David Wilkerson. God knew, though, and wasn't surprised at all. After hope became a noun for me back in Lantana, it felt like God reached down and orchestrated opportunities and boundary-setters in my life that seemed impossible. As I drove through the Holland tunnel and across the Brooklyn bridge to 416 Clinton Avenue, I didn't have a clue what was going to unfold over the next 18 months, but I knew I was driving into my future.

Dave Wilkerson had suggested I finance a larger car, if possible, to haul supplies for my work with Teen Challenge; so I drove to New York in my new Chevy Impala. After a few days of orientation, meetings, and street evangelism, I understood my mission. I was going to travel around the country and preach, but I was also going to share the story of Teen Challenge to congregations and ministers and anyone who would listen. My goal was to raise money to help support a new part of Teen Challenge: God's Mountain.

God's Mountain was a new rehabilitation center sitting on three acres of land only a few hours west of NYC in Rehrersburg, Pennsylvania. With donated farmland in Amish country, Dave built on top of the small hill and called it God's Mountain. His work with troubled teens and drug addicts in New York inspired the idea for a place where youth could rehab with fewer distractions and temporarily enjoy a simpler life on acres of farmland away from the city.

The building held a chapel on one end, a kitchen and dining hall on the other, and in between was enough space to house thirty young men. It was also part of a larger farm where the men could milk cows and learn other farm chores. God's Mountain was my next stop and Frank Reynolds, the director of the program, was my next boundary-setter. As I loaded all the equipment for church meetings into my Impala, I began to see why Dave suggested a larger car. My traveling evangelist supplies included one very large screen to show *The Devil's Pit* (a documentary on the Teen Challenge ministry in New York City), a projector to show the movie, boxes of books to sell, including *The Cross and the Switchblade,* as well as other materials Dave had written, and finally my personal luggage. There was a little bit of room left for maybe two passengers which turned out to be beneficial later on.

I sat in Frank's office and listened to his story. He graduated from Cornell University with plans to be an engineer, but God had other plans and called him to ministry. Frank was one of the most gracious, humble men I had ever met; but as I observed the way he interacted with the young men of God's Mountain, I realized it was his street savvy combined with graciousness and humbleness that allowed him to powerfully connect with and mentor a house full of converted addicts and gang members. He and I agreed that when I traveled and preached, the emphasis should be introducing people to Christ. If I took care of that, God would supply the money. Even though I believed completely in this method and had always lived my life month to month financially, it was difficult to ignore the weight of responsibility placed on my shoulders. God's Mountain needed about $5000 a month to run successfully and only about half of it was raised through promised pledges. I was being called to bridge the gap. With no contacts or experience in fund-raising for new, budding ministries, I wasn't sure how to begin. Most of my experience at Toccoa was under seasoned and established ministries with no real risk involved.

Frank called a friend in upper New York state and asked if I could come to a ministers' retreat to share about Teen Challenge. Hopefully, if I was engaging enough and the Spirit moved hearts, some of them might invite me to speak in their churches. In those days Teen Challenge was a novel and inspiring ministry. No one in Christian circles was actively reaching out to teen gang members and addicts, especially in New York City. Familiar with *The Cross and the Switchblade*, and curious about this new ministry, the friend agreed to give me a ten minute slot in one of the services. I spoke about Teen Challenge and God's Mountain and how God was interested in redeeming everyone, even gang members and drug addicts who might seem unreachable. No one was out of bounds to God. The response was amazing. One pastor invited me to come home with him and preach in his church that Sunday. There was little to no money for restaurants and lodging in those days, so I was grateful for his hospitality.

Several young people came up to me after I spoke at the church and shared that my words changed their lives. I knew they were experiencing God's words, not mine. He was opening a new ministry and using me to do it. The church also took a special offering for Teen Challenge. The offering provided more than enough to cover my travel expenses with leftovers for God's Mountain. That pastor called some of his friends who invited me to their churches. Word of mouth spread and I drove from place to place. For two weeks I preached in the area and God miraculously changed people's lives.

When I returned to Rehrersburg with a good report and cash for the ministry, Frank and I rejoiced. God had spoken clearly: *Proclaim my good news and I will do the rest.* With that as my core value, I never asked for a guaranteed amount of money to speak at a church. I only requested an opportunity for people to respond with an offering for Teen Challenge. Like the story of the little boy with five loaves and two fish, God multiplied and provided more than enough; with baskets of leftovers.

30
MIRACLES

"I'm not riding by myself. You two testimony boys come with me!"

Opportunities to speak and share the story of Teen Challenge grew. I started observing how the real life stories about Teen Challenge really resonated with people; especially the youth. What if I could bring some men from God's Mountain along with me to share their own personal stories? Who better to show the authentic transforming power of Christ than a recovering addict or former gang member? When I proposed this idea to Frank he was intrigued, but doubtful. I was young and inexperienced. What would I do if something went wrong? How could I provide the kind of accountability these men needed while on the road? We eventually agreed on some guidelines, one being that this could serve as a reward for some of the men who had been at God's Mountain for a while and showed strong improvements in recovery. Another guideline was that I only stay on the road for two weeks before returning to Rehrersburg to pick up new guys for the next trip.

Two of the first young men I took on the road were both named Hector, so we drew straws and called one Hector 1, the other Hector 2. Their stories were compelling and I worked with them on sharing their testimonies in 5 to 7 minutes. I crafted three messages to share after the testimonies and rotated these messages as we traveled from venue to venue. As the schedule and routine of being on the road grew more comfortable the guys would ask, "Which three point sermon are you going to give tonight?" There was "Selling Out For A Pot of Stew" which was about Esau and Jacob, "Taking a Stand" featured the three Hebrew Children, and "Are You Ready?" dealt with the second coming of Christ. We listened to each other so frequently that I could give their testimonies and they could preach my messages.

We spoke at churches, schools, Rotary Clubs, even an emerging Christian TV station called CBN in Norfolk, Virginia where Pat Robertson ran a small broadcasting studio. He interviewed us a couple of times and put Teen Challenge's name out there as people watched the program. We stayed in the homes of hospitable and trusting families. People's response was overwhelming and many found a new life in following Christ. For the young men on my team, meeting new people, staying in homes, eating a variety of food, and seeing others moved by their stories added value and depth to their lives.

Church to church, home to home, heart to heart. This became our pattern of ministry. We were the original "couch surfers." We preached and shared the Good News. We sat around generous dinner tables eating warm casseroles and hot bowls of soup. We listened to people's stories and told them ours. In the morning we thanked our gracious hosts for their hospitality and moved on. In late August of 1963, just a couple of months into this new routine, my friend, David Frenchak, asked if I would come to Youngstown, Ohio to meet his pastor Kathryn Kuhlman. Kathryn was an evangelist well known for the amazing healing miracles that happened during her meetings. She lived in Pittsburgh and held a healing service that filled Carnegie Hall every Friday morning. On Sundays she preached in Youngstown to a couple thousand people at the Stambaugh auditorium. Crowds stood in long lines just to hear her speak and be a part of her healing ministry.

Hector 1 and Hector 2 were on the road with me again because of the rotation schedule, so we all met Kathryn Kuhlman on a Sunday in Youngstown. The two Hectors gave testimonies in the youth service and created a buzz throughout the congregation. Miss Kuhlman had heard about David Wilkerson and wanted him to speak at her church as well so I called Dave and connected them. After church she invited the three of us to have dinner with her at her favorite restaurant, located in a small bed and breakfast in Western, PA. As we started toward our car to follow her she pointed at the young men from God's Mountain and said,

"I'm not riding by myself. You two testimony boys come ride with me!"

She bought us steak dinners, put us up in a swanky hotel for the night, and took us shopping the next morning to outfit us in Hickey Freeman suits complete with new shirts, ties, and shoes. We met her staff and had some time to ask Kathryn questions about ministry.

When she learned that the two Hectors wanted to go to Bible School to study, Miss Kuhlman arranged for them to matriculate immediately at Central Bible College in Missouri and set them up with full scholarships. She told me to drive straight there from Pennsylvania and she would cover all expenses. We drove to Missouri and both Hectors enrolled in school that week. I headed back to God's Mountain still trying to make sense of our whirlwind weekend. Kathryn made large donations to God's Mountain and today there is a building there named after her.

Kathryn Kuhlman bought me one of the best steaks I've ever tasted and my very first suit. She gave two Hectors the gift of education. She held healing services every week for years and gave God all the glory every single time; but what made her so impressive was how unimpressed she was with herself. She identified herself as a daughter of God and expressed that believers in Christ were family. As I continued traveling and preaching to support God's Mountain, I began to see how people are connected through sharing their stories, and how the stories all highlight a need for Christ's hope and love in all our lives. I began to see how real ministry is lived out in real people every day. I also began to feel connected to a bigger thing unfolding before me.

In the invitation to enjoy a home-cooked meal or a restaurant quality steak, in the rest and comfort of a guest bed, in the genuine hospitality of gracious people, I experienced a larger invitation to a more generous meal around the ever-expanding table of Christ. I was feasting at His table with His family. Regardless of the details of my life, His table made it possible for me to see others as my brother or sister in Christ whether they be a Godly woman leading a healing service or a recovering drug addict. His table invited us all to share our stories and then marvel at how His story always redeems ours.

31
DIRECTION

"What are your thoughts about the future, Bob?"

I sat comfortably in the Stanphills' living room one winter evening and considered the loaded question. All the possible directions my life could take felt like a multi-forked intersection with no map. All of them were good, but each would lead me to a very different place. Did I want to stay in Teen Challenge and continue preaching as a traveling evangelist? Was God calling me to grow as a leader through the pursuit of further education? Could I do both? Where would I find the right kind of schooling? How did dating and marrying fit into all this? These were all questions stacked neatly inside one another like Russian nesting dolls and Ira Stanphill had just asked the biggest one that housed all the others, "What are your thoughts about the future?"

As my traveling ministry with Teen Challenge had increased I began to ask myself how long I wanted to do this. Ira and Gloria Stanphill, who I had met back in Lantana with Paul and Audrey Davis, had eventually moved to pastor a church in Lancaster, Pennsylvania about one hour from God's Mountain. Ira invited me to preach at his church one Sunday in February and I gladly came. During a conversation after the service he encouraged me to make some time for personal care and rest or I would burn out. He even offered his home as a respite if I ever wanted to stay longer. I agreed that this was a good idea and returned back to Lancaster for some R&R a few weeks later. I was weary from being on the road and keeping such an intense speaking schedule.

At Toccoa one of my favorite professors, "Pop" Lindsay, was an alumnus of Wheaton College and frequently shared stories about his time there and its graduate school. Because of this I became enamored with Wheaton College and dreamed of maybe applying there someday to further my education. I learned they offered an M.A. in New Testament Studies that sounded interesting. Ira knew about my desire to pursue more education at Wheaton because of a previous conversation we had while I was at Toccoa. I had also told him about my communication with Dr. Tenney, the Dean of Wheaton Graduate School. When I contacted him about applying to the school, Dr. Tenney suggested I receive a degree from a regionally accredited college before applying to Wheaton, since Toccoa only had Bible College accreditation at the time. I was just starting to consider when and how to begin that process.

While staying with the Stanphills for some rest, they invited a young lady in the church over for dinner one night with my permission. Not only did they admire this girl and her family, but her dad happened to be Academic Dean at Elizabethtown College, which was nearby. Ira and Gloria were secretly hoping for a match made in heaven and maybe the perfect connection for my bachelor's degree too. We all had a nice evening and talked about Elizabethtown College or E-town as all the locals called it, but nothing special sparked between the young lady and me.

I continued traveling and raising money for God's Mountain. I enjoyed living out of a suitcase, navigating the challenge of a new place, and feeling like my life had purpose; but I also kept thinking about more education. The question Ira had asked kept circling in my mind ... *what are your thoughts about the future?* Summer months were slower and many churches didn't bring in special speakers until the fall, so I decided to stay at God's Mountain for lodging and register for one class at E-town to test the academic waters. I had to drive about an hour to the college, but I could also still speak occasionally throughout the summer. Frank Reynolds approved and thought it was a good idea to get some more education.

As I stood in line waiting to register for the history course I chose to take that summer I recognized someone. Joanie Hershman, the girl I met at the Stanphills' home for dinner back in early March, was standing in line just ahead of me. She was enrolled at E-town, of course, since her dad was the Academic Dean. She recognized me too and we made small talk as the line slowly moved forward. I asked her to get a cup of coffee afterward and we mostly discussed classes and student life as well as life in Lancaster. We parted and wished each other well with school as I still had some ministry to finish out before the summer session started. Our time together was comfortable and friendly, and taking a class at E-town somehow seemed a little more attractive to me now. Maybe I was headed in the right direction.

32
POSSIBILITIES

"Where am I going to sleep? Where am I going to eat?
I can't go there."

Ben stared at me with a puzzled, hurt look in his eyes. I was stunned that I hadn't even thought about this. I was so moved by all the amazing possibilities and transformations I had witnessed in people's lives around the country that I hadn't even considered the horrible truth Ben faced every day. I had asked Ben, a recovering addict who was thriving at God's Mountain, to travel with me and share his story. I was especially excited about this trip because Toccoa was one of the stops and I was scheduled to speak at my alma mater. Ben was a little older than the average age of young men recovering at God's Mountain. He was a refined, educated young man from Detroit who had fallen into addiction. He was also black and personally understood some ugly realities I didn't. Even though it was 1964, for many communities south of the Mason Dixon line, racial equality was still considered just an idea written on paper. Until it was written on people's hearts, this was a barrier, particularly in the South. Ben was a recovering addict, but the color of his skin was much more concerning to white southern communities. Even the Church struggled to bridge that gap.

My enthusiasm over God's work in Ben's life blinded me to the ugly discrimination that was a sad reality in so many places. We cried together when we realized it would not be in his best interest to force this issue right now. I still carry a remnant of that grief when I think about Ben's pain and all the missed possibilities from that decision. It had been years since the childhood bike crash in Olustee where two little boys retreated from each other to keep peace; and even more years since war tore a country apart over many disagreements, one being the emancipation of slaves. The kind of life one lived and individual privileges based solely on skin color was still very much a battle in 1964. Sadly, it was evident in the church as much as the neighborhoods. I knew that the only answer to this healing was Jesus and the power of his Good News. Only Jesus' power to reconcile each of us to God and change our hearts would bring true reconciliation among people, regardless of skin color. There was work to be done and I felt called more than ever to continue this work through ministry. Maybe it was possible that a day was coming where the Bens of the world would be welcomed with open hearts everywhere.

As I struggled with real and current day to day problems, I also wrestled with discerning God's call on my life for the future. Traveling for Teen Challenge and growing as an evangelist and Christian leader had definitely been the right decision. Frank poured hours of time into mentoring me and connecting me with so many people in ministry. The life-changing experiences and opportunities I fully embraced paved an intriguing road of possibility, but strangely I felt like my time at God's Mountain was nearing an end. A desire to push forward and pursue more education burned slowly inside me like the embers of a blazing fire slowing down.

Right before I took a summer course at E-town, a friend from my Toccoa days invited me to speak at his church. He planned and organized a five day crusade in Ft. Wayne, Indiana where he was on staff. The whole congregation spent time praying and fasting for this week of meetings. More people than we'd ever witnessed became Christ followers that week. We couldn't explain it. There was nothing different from those services other than the intentional praying and fasting beforehand. The only explanation that made sense was God showed up in a miraculous way and transformed lives. Afterwards we referred to it as the "Ft Wayne Happening." Maybe God was starting even then to show me that the deepest, richest possibilities lay only in a life dedicated to knowing him and depending on him for everything. Maybe I needed to fully trust where he wanted to lead me.

By the fall of 1964 after praying, talking, thinking, and praying some more, I enrolled in Elizabethtown College as a full-time student to work on a bachelor's degree. The summer course went well and I knew this was the next step for me. Ira Stanphill was looking for a youth pastor to hire and offered me the position. Being a youth pastor could help me develop new ministry skills and afford me the flexible schedule I needed as a student. I let Frank Reynolds and David Wilkerson know about my plans and we agreed that December would be my last official month with Teen Challenge. A family from Ira's church offered me a room at their house, free of charge, while I was earning my degree and running the youth program at First Assembly of God. They bought new bedroom furniture and fixed up the room just for me. I was surprised and touched by their generosity. The furniture was beautiful and more extravagant than anything I'd ever had.

A new season in my life was beginning. The routine of a school year, ministering in a church environment, and coming home to the same room every night slowed me down and settled me. It allowed me to ponder possibilities for the future. One of the biggest possibilities I didn't really consider at the time was my friendship with Joanie Hershman. She attended First Assembly and was on the youth group planning team so we spent a lot of time together and enjoyed each other's company. I had no idea our friendship would grow into something more. I had no idea her family would accept me as one of their own. I had no idea she would change my life forever.

33
EXPANDED

"I have one question for you".

I sat in front of Dr. Jake Hershman and felt absolutely rattled.

"Can you support her mom and me in our old age?"

Only a moment passed, but it felt like ten, before he broke out in laughter and said, "Welcome to the family, Bob. I give you and Joanie my blessing to get married." I had been living in Lancaster and was enjoying the youth pastor position. Classes at Elizabethtown were moving me toward a Bachelor's Degree with Philosophy and Religion as my declared major. With the introduction of so many new thoughts and ideas, my worldview expanded.

The Bomberger family provided complimentary housing for me and created an incredible "home" experience. They invited me to be a part of their family whenever I wanted, including family meals and trips. After Granny died, I grew skilled at the nomadic life and learning how to thrive in different settings. I lived in Jacksonville and Lantana with the Drydens, several college roommates at Toccoa, scores of different homes as I traveled for Teen Challenge, and now a new family in Lancaster. I grew into more of an understanding about all the ways God shows us what family and community look like. Granny's love and commitment to care for me was a powerful example of what family does for each other. Complete strangers committing to love and care for me was a powerful example of what the family of God does for each other. Both of these examples integrated and grew in my heart. My understanding of family and home expanded.

Joanie Hershman became more than a friend after many meetings, rides home, and a few impromptu meals out. We started dating in March and fell in love. One foggy night as I was driving her home we came to the railroad crossing near her house. The flashing lights signaled to stop, but no gate came down. We waited and waited. After a while we figured something had malfunctioned so I drove up the small incline to cross the tracks. As we started across Joanie screamed, "Bob!" The light from a locomotive engine broke through the fog and was bearing down on us. Panicking, I floored it, but the tracks were slick and icy from the remains of a Pennsylvania winter and the car's tires spun, struggling to gain traction. There wasn't time to even think about what was happening. Before either of us could say a thing, we felt the car lurch forward violently and the next thing we knew our car was somehow, miraculously, on the other side of the tracks. We were shaken, but unharmed. The train should have plowed straight into us, but instead something had pushed us off the tracks.

We both knew it had been a close call and were fairly silent the rest of the drive. When we got to the house, I checked the back of the car. There was a small piece of the bumper missing, like someone had taken a scoop out of it. Joanie's mother met us at the door and asked "Are you two all right?" She had been asleep when something woke her and she felt the sudden urge to pray for us. We told her what happened. The three of us joined hands and thanked God for His protection. To this day, we believe an angel pushed us across the tracks and spared our lives. Our trust in God expanded.

I asked permission to marry Joanie and survived her Dad's idea of a funny joke. The first time I asked her to marry me was on a warm, late summer night in a Lancaster park, on a small bridge overlooking a bubbling brook. I had a fake ring and purposely fumbled with the ring so it flipped into the brook, which was my idea of a funny joke. Joanie burst into tears and I immediately realized proposals were no laughing matter. I assured her I had the real ring in my pocket and pulled it out; this time I steadied my hand and slid the ring on her finger. We kissed and I was genuinely relieved that she said "yes" after my shenanigans. We were married the following January in the middle of a snowstorm. None of my relatives could make it so we traveled to Florida for part of our honeymoon and Joanie met my family for the first time.

Aunt Inez cooked up a big southern feast for dinner our first night in Florida. Everything was delicious and the visit went well. Aunt Inez told me privately how much she liked Joan. My new bride was a great conversationalist and got along with everyone so there were no awkward moments. Well, maybe one. Aunt Inez and Uncle E.D. retired early and we told them we were going to stay up and talk or go grab a cup of coffee, but we'd be sure to lock up and turn the lights out. When we finally went to bed we were both exhausted from the long day. Joan was already in bed when I crawled across her to get to my side. The room was small and the bed was pushed against the wall. All of a sudden the whole bed collapsed with a loud crack. We were startled and both scrambled to get out of the mess. Aunt Inez and E.D. came running in and apologized profusely.

"We're so sorry. We have trouble with that bed and the slats slipping off the frame. We'll help you fix it."

With their help, I placed the slats under the mattress and put the bed back together. Joan was mortified and wondered what my aunt and uncle must have imagined with newly weds in their guest bed. It took some time before she could laugh about it.

Traveling home from our honeymoon we hit another snowstorm and barely made it to a hotel. As I stood in line, waiting to check in at the front desk, the customer in front of me turned and asked if I had a wife.

"A new one," I grinned and held up my hand with the wedding ring, "just married!"

He let us take the last room. The motel owner invited the gracious gentleman to stay in his house for the night. The next morning as we counted our coins at the restaurant, a waitress came over. "Are you short on money?" she asked. We explained we were on our honeymoon and got stranded in the snowstorm.

"Order whatever you want, it's on the house," she replied with a wink. Our picture of generosity expanded.

Joanie and I both finished a final spring and summer semester at E-town, graduated, and moved to Illinois in late August for me to start a Master's program at Wheaton. I was humbled by how God continued to work in my life. The classes at Wheaton challenged me while molding and shaping my mind. Joanie got a job teaching first grade and put all she learned about elementary education into practice. The friendships we formed with other married grad students created a sense of family which was wonderful since we were both far from home. Married life took us on the typical ups and downs of learning how to put someone else's needs ahead of your own. We worked on knowing and understanding each other through day to day life, and the space that held our differences became smaller and smaller, as understanding and consideration toward one another grew and expanded to make enough room for a life together.

34
DISTRACTIONS

"Do you think God has changed his mind?"

I remember how this question cut deeply to the heart of the matter. Joan and I settled into grad school life. We rented a small apartment and Joan taught while I attended classes and worked multiple jobs. We started attending Wheaton First Assembly of God with new friends and became youth sponsors. When the pastor resigned, the board appointed me as the interim pastor during the summer of '67. I considered submitting my name to be the lead pastor. Dr. Cooley attended the church and was also one of my professors. I decided to talk with him about whether or not to pursue being pastor of this church.

"Bob, why did you come to Wheaton?" he quietly asked me after I explained the situation.

"To get a masters degree in New Testament," I responded with conviction.

"Do you think God has changed his mind?"

The room silently held the weight of the truth and wisdom in his question.

"No,"...I answered reflectively.

Dr. Cooley continued and suggested that if I became the pastor I would be distracted and probably never complete my degree. That conversation helped fine tune my ability to recognize that even good opportunities can distract from what God is doing in one's heart and mind. It was a hard decision because I loved the leadership aspect of pastoring, especially the preaching role. However, I immediately resigned as interim pastor and helped usher the following Sunday to show my continued support for the church.

Shortly before I finished course work at Wheaton, a man in the church offered me an extremely attractive sales job that promised a six figure salary within three years. Joan and I needed the money. I was finishing classes and beginning my thesis. Joan was teaching and pregnant with our first child, but we both wanted her to be able to stay home with the baby. While I was pondering all of this, he called back and said he was taking the offer off the table.

"I don't want to be responsible for keeping you from the ministry God is preparing for you," he explained.

I was disappointed at the time but recognized the situation as yet another distraction.

On a hot, midwestern summer day in July of '68 we packed all our belongings and headed for Alexandria, Virginia where Joan's parents lived now. We decided it would help to live near family with a baby on the way. I spoke with David Wilkerson and agreed to travel again for Teen Challenge. This time I would raise money to start Teen Challenge centers in Europe. I could base myself out of Alexandria for a year and hopefully head to Europe with my family after that. After two weeks of traveling and preaching I sensed that even though it felt familiar, something had shifted inside me. My heart wasn't in this ministry like it had been before. I had a wife and was about to become a father. I had no idea what to expect and wondered about my fatherless childhood. What kind of father would I be?

Joan missed me and struggled without me there even though she had family nearby. I flew home in the middle of the two weeks to visit, and we both experienced clarity. In my New Testament studies at Wheaton, I learned about "kairos," the Greek word for perfect timing or the right moment. Joan and I had a kairos moment during that short visit. We knew God wasn't calling us to Teen Challenge. The thought of traveling to Europe with a new baby was overwhelming for both of us and we had no peace about it. With one phone call, I resigned from Teen Challenge. I told David I felt like God was preparing me to be a pastor. He understood and wished me well. I finished my preaching commitments, then returned home and looked for a job to support my family.

I had been a successful evangelist and was close to completing my Master's thesis; but for the first time in a while, I had no idea what came next. No means of income. No sudden impression to move one way or another. No boundary-setter speaking into my life. I felt like that little boy in Olustee, crossing the trestle and hoping to beat a train. Financial security had never worried me much, but now, loud and steady, it was bearing down on me like a locomotive. I was responsible for my wife and a child. It was harder to trust God for my family than for myself. I thought of all the ways God had provided for me in my life. I knew He was still in charge; we just needed to trust Him and be obedient and patient.

Through a family connection I started working at a furniture store and for little more than minimum wage helped deliver furniture, which barely provided for our needs. The other workers joked about needing a master's degree to make the weekly trip to the landfill where we dumped the trash that accumulated at the store. It was a humbling experience. Should we have stayed in Wheaton and pastored? Or worked sales and enjoyed a comfortable lifestyle? What was God doing and why did He suddenly seem so silent?

During my six months at the furniture store I occasionally preached on the weekends. With no insurance, the honorariums helped pay the medical expenses when our first child, Julie, was born. I see now how God used this time in our lives as a transition. Transitions are hard and often unexciting. They can be overwhelming and underwhelming at the same time. You are between two things and the space feels undefined. Joan and I learned how to parent a newborn. We learned how to trust God to daily provide for our family. We learned how to live between the known and the unknown.

As we fasted and prayed for God to open a door for me to pastor, twelve people in Richmond, Virginia fasted and prayed for God to send the right pastor for a new church they were planning. God was on the move. Despite our distractions and questions and transitions, God was on the move.

35
BEGINNINGS

"When can we start having public services?"

I glanced at Joan and she gave me a knowing look. God had been preparing us. It wouldn't be easy. There was no guarantee of anything, only a soaring feeling of obedience mixed with anticipation. We recognized God's voice and the Holy Spirit's insistent nudge. Maybe this was the beginning we had been waiting for.

A few weeks earlier Joan and I left the baby with grandparents for the day and drove two hours south to Richmond, Virginia to meet with a group of twelve people gathered in a home basement. Joan's uncle was an official in the Assemblies of God and knew of this group in Richmond looking to find a pastor and start a church. He encouraged us to interview. We agreed and drove down on a cold afternoon in early January, 1969.

"The twelve," as they called themselves, were four families and a few individuals who had diligently planned and prayed until they were finally approved to start a new church in the affluent West End of Richmond. Joan and I were younger than almost everyone in the group by twenty years, and I knew very little about starting a church. However, I was energetic about sharing the Gospel with people. My Teen Challenge experience and leading the youth ministry for Ira Stanphill provided me with practical training in all sorts of areas. My education piqued the group's interest, and I shared my vision and ideas about leading a pentecostal church. I believed a combination of clear Biblical teaching, anointed worship through singing, and orderly expressions of spiritual gifts could foster and grow hearts to reach the world with the Good News. My age and inexperience with church planting did not seem to concern the twelve. They thought my vision matched theirs for a new Assemblies of God church in the area. They believed God would provide the finances to hire a full time pastor and asked me to consider the call to Richmond.

The meeting ended with prayer and we all agreed to take the next two weeks to fast and pray about this ministry opportunity. On the drive home Joan and I talked. Joan felt concerned about whether or not we would be a good fit based on the ultra conservative reputation of the Assembly of God churches in the Potomac District. How would that affect my unconventional approach as a budding evangelist? We both felt unsure about the resources of a small, beginner church and its ability to financially support our family. At the same time we both felt the pull of a new exciting ministry full of promise. I wondered if another twelve people, thousands of years ago, felt the same way as they began the messy business of forming not just a church, but The Church. Could Joan and I begin this beginning with a huge step of faith? Could we trust God to provide and make a way when it wasn't easy? Was it possible to question and doubt, yet remain open and willing at the same time? Was God our hope even when we weren't sure about the future?

After prayer, fasting, and many conversations with family and people we considered mentors, colleagues, or close friends, we drove back to Richmond. The air was thick with anticipation from the twelve. After letting them know we would come if they wanted us, we left the room while they took a vote. They brought us back in and everyone stood.

"We unanimously voted for you to be our pastor. When can we start having public services?" the spokesperson announced.

We grinned and started hugging each other as brothers and sisters in Christ. From that moment on there was never a plan B. There was only God's plan. My salary was based on a private poll taken among the twelve earlier before we met. On an index card, each one anonymously wrote down an amount they felt they could give each week. When the amounts were added, the group made a faith decision to raise it by $30 and trusted that God would provide what they couldn't.

We set the date for West End Assembly of God's (WEAG) first official service on Sunday, March 2, 1969. It snowed six inches that morning, but 42 people braved their way to the Executive Motor Hotel where we rented space to meet. One person became a Christ-follower and the offering was $242.00 which more than covered our first paycheck. Possibility and faith, gratefulness and relief filled our hearts in layers like the gentle, yet steady snow. A beginning had begun.

36
ENOUGH

"We thought it was best for Bobby."

Right after Joan and I said yes to starting a church in Richmond, Virginia, we took some time to drive down to Florida and visit Uncle E.D. and Aunt Inez. We had visited twice, but this time we were bringing our new baby, Julie, and couldn't wait for them to meet her. We knew once we started ministry in Richmond, we wouldn't be able to get away for a while.

Joan was feeling more comfortable with my family and the southern culture in North Florida, but she was curious and still asked a lot of questions about my upbringing, particularly around Harold Rhoden's absence in my life. I had told her all I knew and assured her that my life with Granny was simple, but very loving. It was sad that my parents divorced and I never knew either of them, but I didn't really think about it much since Granny's death and my leaving home for school and ministry. On the trip down to Lake City Joan posed another question.

"Don't you think it's strange that you don't know anything about Harold and that he never got in touch with you after you met him at the hospital? I mean, you share his name. I have this strange feeling that there's something missing from your story."

Honestly, I didn't think it was strange at all until she mentioned it. I felt confused and hurt that Harold didn't reach out after I met him as a teenager, but now I just thought Harold probably wasn't that great of a guy. I guess I figured my family would tell me if there was more to the story. I thought all this in my head, but what I said was, "Well, we're heading to the perfect place to find out. I can ask Aunt Inez during our visit." Joan seemed to like that idea and went back to playing with Julie. I was beginning to understand how to better navigate the relational part of marriage: don't say the very first thing that pops into your head!

We had a great visit with Aunt Inez and Uncle E.D. They both loved meeting Julie and she entertained everyone in her own baby way. One afternoon as we were sitting around, talking and catching up, I brought up my family history and mentioned Harold Rhoden. I mentioned that becoming a parent caused Joan and me to wonder more about my parents and asked Aunt Inez if she could tell me anything about Harold Rhoden or even maybe how to contact him. She looked down for a minute, then sighed and said, "Bobby, I guess you're old enough to know the whole story now. Harold Rhoden isn't your father."

No one moved or said a word as the air tried to support that heavy sentence. She continued, "There was a young man named Drew Strickland who worked on the farm for Granny. Drew and Martha liked each other. Drew is your father."

"What about Harold?" I asked quietly. "Who was Harold?"

Aunt Inez nodded and continued. "Drew took off once Martha was pregnant. Didn't want to be tied down. Harold lived in town and knew your mom. He married her right before she gave birth to you so everything would be proper. She named you after him. Harold did a good thing for our family, but he and Martha were young and their marriage didn't last long."

I didn't have any words to say. Everything I believed about my beginning was wrong. I thought all this time that Harold was my biological dad and just didn't want to know me. It made sense now, why he never got in touch with me after we met at the hospital. We weren't related. We weren't father and son. We only shared a name.

"Do you know how I can get in touch with Drew now? I'd like to at least meet him."

Aunt Inez shook her head. "We heard Drew died years ago." She whispered the word "died" like it was a bad word. I had heard my relatives do this for years at family gatherings. Anything having to do with death was always whispered in the Cobb family. She continued, "He was young, maybe 30. Somethin' about his heart. He had a weak heart."

Joan cleared her throat and tried to make sense of the scrambled story. "So Martha Lee Cobb, Bob's mother, got pregnant by Drew Strickland, a hired farm hand. Drew left town and right before Bob was born, a friend of Martha's, Harold Rhoden, married her to give the child a name. Harold and Martha divorced a year later. Then Martha married Ashley Weeks and both of them were hit and killed by a drunk driver one night. Martha was only 17 when she died. Granny raised Bob from the age of two until he was 12 and told him Harold was his father. Then Bob came and lived with you all and continued to believe that Harold was his father. An uncle even took him to meet Harold while Granny was in the hospital. And not one person in the family thought to tell him the whole story until right now?"

Aunt Inez nodded and said, "We thought it was best for Bobby."

I don't remember much about the rest of the visit. My story was a lot to process. I didn't feel angry with anyone, just stunned and surprised. I never expected Aunt Inez to say that Harold Rhoden wasn't my father. Joan and I talked about it on the long drive home. She was a great listener and empathized with me about my shock over learning this pivotal piece of family history. I was used to working things out alone, in my head; so talking about it with a spouse was new for me, but it felt comforting to share my thoughts with someone who loved and cared for me so deeply. We both agreed that for now, it was enough just to know the truth.

We had each other and extended family. We had a baby to love and raise. We had a new congregation and ministry to nurture. We had more life before us than behind us.

For now the truth was enough.

37
GRIT

"You work your side of the street and I'll work mine!"

I sat in a meeting with ministers from different churches around the area and tried to mask my stunned expression as an awkward silence followed the comment. It wasn't the first time I had experienced this type of hurtful attitude and it wouldn't be the last. After giving an update on WEAG (West End Assembly of God) and sharing the good things we were experiencing as a congregation, an older minister responded with this terse comment. I chose not to respond, but wondered how I would be accepted in the clergy if I was only seen as "the competition." We were supposed to be a group of supportive colleagues celebrating and commiserating with each others' ministry stories. However, the disappointing reality was that some pastors viewed other churches as competition. I learned over the years that real competition for the church is not the church down the street, but any alternative activity that steals people's use of time.

Because of my experience with Teen Challenge, doors opened for me to speak around Richmond, and WEAG became known in the area quickly. Even though we were still meeting in the rented location downtown, the congregation set a vision for how WEAG could serve Richmond. We committed to planting churches in a circle around Richmond over time. I didn't know how it would all come together, but I was doing what I knew how to do best - putting my head down, getting the work done, and trusting God for the rest. Somehow, this pattern of doing the natural, and leaving the supernatural up to God, worked well for me. If I remained willing to be used, he always found ways to use me for his glory. Even at times when I felt used up, God renewed me in unique ways. One of these ways was gently prodding my memory back to the days when I lived with Granny and we had next to nothing. Her faith in God and the plans he had for me traveled with me in memory. Some days, even though it had been years since Granny died, I could still hear her voice. "Bobby, I love you and God loves you. Always follow God."

Moving out of the Executive Motor Hotel into a building of our own became a primary goal for the congregation. As we began searching for land to build in the West End of town, Floyd Beach, one of the twelve, called and gave me the name of a realtor he had seen in the paper. I arranged a meeting with the realtor, but he never showed. Having experienced a direct approach in conflict-resolution with a variety of mentors, I followed up with a call and asked the realtor if it was his practice to stand up his clients. After a moment of stunned silence, he answered, "No, but the reality is you probably need someone to give you some land. You really can't afford anything in the West End." He suggested contacting Julia Robins, a lady known for her philanthropy and who happened to own acres of land in the West End. Apparently, we didn't just need land, we needed a miracle, or two!

My first meeting with Julia Robins was the type of experience I had only read about. As I turned off Sleepy Hollow Road with its lazy bends and curves and drove through the parted black iron gates with "Raleigh" scrolled across the center, I was stunned by the beautiful 40 acre estate. I passed a serene lake surrounded by perfectly manicured gardens and pulled up to a sprawling, classic brick house in the middle of a wooded setting. The housekeeper, Mattie, met me at the door and escorted me to the library where I sat on a couch in a room that was windowed on one side with a beautiful view of the lake. The house smelled of old wood, lemon polish, and savory dishes cooked so many times that a signature smell seemed baked into the walls. Once I was settled with a coke and some cookies, Mattie ushered in Mrs Robins. She was thin and of medium height with silvery hair worn in a traditional style for women over 60. Stately elegance shimmered around her like a physical presence, and I stood quickly when she extended her hand, introduced herself, and said, "Nice to meet you."

From a straight back chair at a small antique desk, she asked me questions about myself and the church we wanted to build. I learned that her husband had died of heart failure a few years earlier. Her raspy voice held a distinct cadence that I later learned to identify as "old Richmond". Her southern phrases, such as "bless your heart," softened her proper sentences and despite her widowed state she was savvy and knew a lot about me because she had done research through one of her pastor friends in town. Mrs. Robins suggested I speak with her business manager and look at some property.

"Pick out three acres," she said, which was the minimum the county required for a church. I thanked her and asked if I could pray with her before I left. She agreed.

In the end we offered to buy three acres from her and held our breath for her response. On New Year's Eve, 1969, she called me to her house and said, " If you can get this transaction notarized before midnight I will gift you the property on Parham Road for the church." With some grit, sacrifice, and a lot of help, we moved heaven and earth to get those papers notarized and delivered to the downtown post office to be postmarked before midnight. Our miracle came in the form of three acres of prime real estate we never could have afforded in Richmond's elite West End. We moved into 501 Parham Road three years later. The congregation gave thanks for this unbelievable turn of events and humbly carried the overwhelming sense that God's presence was with us more than we ever expected or deserved.

38

BEYOND AMAZING

Average attendance on Sundays: 60

Water baptisms: 8

Weddings: 2

Home visits: 50

First time visitors: 185

Sermons preached: 80

Spirit baptisms: 5

Conversions: 4

Hospital visits: 88

Miles put on car: 23,000

This was some of the information listed in the minutes of our first annual business meeting which was actually a 10 month report, not even one year. There were 21 members present. Even with a miraculous start, church planting took hard work, long hours, and unfortunately, some neglect of my family. Once we secured the land we needed, figuring out how to fund the building was our next hurdle. We couldn't borrow enough money in a conventional way so we sold church bonds, a non-guaranteed promissory note between the individual and the church. We set a budget and hired an architect to draw up blueprints for a contemporary-style building. We hoped to save on labor costs by using volunteers from the congregation where appropriate, but still, we were $25,000.00 over our $100,000.00 budget. One evening, we held a meeting with the congregation and architect. Could we get approval to move forward with the extra cost? The architect was doubtful.

After the budget and building presentation, a lady in the congregation stood and shared a scripture she felt the Lord put on her heart. In I Chronicles 22:14-16 David says, "I have taken great pains to provide for the temple of the Lord a hundred thousand talents ... you may add to them. ... You have many workmen. ... Now begin the work and the Lord be with you." After all these years I can still picture the architect's face, mouth hanging open, as people in the congregation nodded heads and affirmed this bold statement with "yeses" and " amens." I must admit I was stunned as well. The vote was 100% for moving ahead with the extra cost and believing God would provide the rest along the way.

The octagonal-shaped chapel that housed a sanctuary in the round at 501 Parham Road became a symbol of God being with us. We moved in November of '72 and Ira Stanphill came to speak at the dedication. Joan and I were so excited to see him again and proudly showed him around the new church building as well as Richmond. He was like a father to me, and now that I too was a father, I appreciated all he'd done for me in a whole new way.

The chapel sanctuary could only seat 125 people, but with folding chairs we pushed it up to 200 and prayed the fire marshall stayed far away. Over the next few years as we caught the wave of the charismatic movement and the Jesus movement that rolled from region to region throughout the United States, our Sunday services grew from one to four. I felt in over my head trying to lead this rapid growth, but continued to say "yes" to God and watched him do great things.

One day I was standing in the center of our chapel, looking around at the floor to ceiling triangular windows that served as our walls in the sanctuary. Looking outside at all God's creation was a beautiful way to worship. Suddenly, a buried memory surfaced and I was nine years old again, back in Olustee, squatting down over the train tracks on the way to Mr. Kirkland's. I remembered tracing the triangular symbol etched in the cross tie, and a promise I had made myself many years ago.

"My life is going to be different someday. I'll remember this day forever. Forever."

This time when I felt filled up from the soles of my feet to the tips of my ears, I knew it wasn't the promise I'd made myself, but the presence of the Holy Spirit filling me with promise. I dropped to my knees, right there in the middle of the sanctuary, lifted my hands, and cried, "God, you are beyond amazing."

39
WELCOMED

"Are you ready?"

Two women sat in the front seat of a car. Waiting. One voiced the question, the other answered with the click of the door handle. Eva and Mary stepped out of the car and walked toward the building. Would they be welcomed? Or turned away?

WEAG had been in their own building for almost two years now. Every Tuesday morning the ladies held a prayer meeting. Eva and Mary had heard about this church and the Tuesday morning prayer meeting. They wanted to be involved, but wondered about fitting in. Would the ladies at WEAG be open to new faces? What if those faces were brown? Even though reconciliation between whites and blacks had improved some by the mid-seventies, there was still plenty of tension in the nation's cities. These two ladies still had every reason to be nervous about how they would be received by a new church located in a predominantly white area of town. They decided to drive to the church together for support, but once they parked, they shut the car off and just waited quietly, gathering courage. Putting on their brave faces and hoping that they wouldn't have to keep them on for long. The minutes ticked by.

As they walked slowly toward the unusual octagonal-shaped building with a folded roof and up the steps to the front door, they held hands and breathed deeply one last time. The door was heavy, but once inside it was only a short walk to the sanctuary. Elaine, the one who led the prayer group, spotted the two visitors right away and welcomed them with a big smile and open arms as they tentatively approached. Elaine was one of the original twelve who started WEAG and she never knew a stranger. Her comfortable, warm, and welcoming spirit put Eva and Mary at ease right away. The other women in the room took Elaine's lead and made space for the new ladies to sit with them.

When Joan shared this account later that evening over dinner, I wondered if this was what true reconciliation looked like. Maybe it was one huge idea made up of small moments, gracious welcoming over and over again until there was no more fear, only love. Maybe sitting together and worshipping together fostered a kind of healing. A healing that was only possible when we threw our hearts wide open to welcome and make room for the Redeemer, and within that sacred act we understood how to make room for each other. I thought of Ben, who wasn't welcome in the South during my years of traveling with Teen Challenge. I thought of how Eva and Mary must have felt walking into a room of all white ladies. I thought about the courage it takes to make a real change.

Eva and Mary came back the next week. And the next. Within the month they decided to start coming on Sunday mornings and eventually became wonderful, active members of our church community. There was more to be done, but change was in the air; and I was more than ready to welcome it graciously. Christ came to reconcile. How could we do anything else but follow his lead?

40
PLANTING

"I've never seen anything like this in Atlantic City!"

While WEAG's first building was under construction, so was my family. Having the first baby was practically effortless. An easy pregnancy, a mild-tempered and flexible child, and a comfortable ratio of two parents to one child. We thought we should definitely have some more. However, with Joan's second pregnancy, everything was different. At the six month check up we found out she was dilating way too early and would need a procedure and complete bed rest until the baby was born. Three months of bed rest! How were we supposed to take care of a new toddler? We were two hours from any extended family. One of us kept unpredictable hours during the days and evenings, and the other was ordered to stay in bed. It felt like God had just planted us in the wilderness with very few provisions.

Julie, our toddler, was my partner in crime and attended meetings with me during the day. Along with my papers and calendar, I now also carried a bag of cheerios, extra diapers, a few toys, and a sippy cup everywhere I went. I was doubtful about this arrangement, but grew to enjoy my little companion, and she seemed content to accompany me anywhere. I don't doubt that many of those meetings probably had a better outcome because of the cute baby I carted around. I became more comfortable with not only the title of dad, but the real connection a father and child can share even in the youngest years. I wondered if this was how my mother felt about me?

Friends and church members showed up with food, gifts, and some even stayed to complete laundry or do some light house cleaning. Joan's parents helped out and kept Julie for a while. Joan read a lot of books and learned to knit while I became an expert on laundry, cooking, and changing diapers. Manna was provided in the wilderness every day. God walked us through a season of depending on Him in a new way and by the middle of March, our son, Robert John, came barrelling into the world.

By the time Joan was pregnant with our third child we prayed that she would not need the procedure and bedrest again; however, at her six month checkup the doctor recommended the same orders. We were disappointed, but knew God would be with us and care for us in unexpected ways wherever we were planted. Cynthia Anne was born in April of '72 and by November of that same year, we were holding church services in our new building. The wilderness felt more like a young, beautiful garden after much waiting and trusting and growth.

By now we had three children and understood first hand the challenges that young parents face every day: lack of sleep, lack of knowledge, lack of having any time to yourself. After two years in our building, WEAG was reaching over two hundred in attendance each week. A small group of people who lived in Mechanicsville, a rural suburb, were driving forty minutes one way to attend. We began discussing a church plant. Even though this was one of our primary goals, we were surprised it happened so quickly.

By June of '74, we launched Mechanicsville Christian Center with about fifty people. I'll never forget the slight panic of that first Sunday when we were thirty people down in attendance at WEAG. What if we couldn't support ourselves anymore? What if all the talent and leadership we gave to the new plant couldn't be replaced? We knew it was the right thing to do, but the reality of sowing generously gave me pause. I had always been a risk taker, willing to try new things, but church planting created another layer of depending on God in a new way. Sometimes God calls you to be planted. Other times God calls you to plant. Either way, it's all his harvest.

Joan and I had the opportunity three years later to spend a weekend in Atlantic City as ecumenical guests of a regional Catholic gathering. It was 1977 and the Charismatic Catholic Movement was under way. Father Danny Mannen, a Catholic priest and friend of mine from Richmond, had invited us to be a part of this special weekend. Not only were we honored at the invitation, we were excited for a little time away from the busy season of raising a family and a church. One evening we found ourselves sitting in a restaurant in Atlantic City with new friends from the conference and when our waitress came to drop off the bill, she exclaimed, "I've never seen anything like this!"

She was referring to the energy, excitement, and transformation filling the city - people walking down the boardwalk with arms linked and singing, "there is a river of life flowing out from me...," praying before meals, speaking kind words to waitstaff in restaurants. It was a joyful atmosphere; but in the middle of all the joy there was a sad moment when the leadership of the Catholic Church had to request that non-catholic ecumenical guests refrain from communion on Sunday morning. Almost everyone wept including the leaders who had to make the announcement. We all prayed that someday it would be different. Someday all would be reconciled.

On the way home I thought about WEAG. In spite of sending a group of strong members to the recent church plant, new people came and filled the gap. We were growing again. Maybe it was time for WEAG to foster "transformation" for the city of Richmond. I wondered about creating an ecumenical gathering in the city around Pentecost. Joan and I had never experienced such an open, accepting gathering like the one in Atlantic City where different denominations came together and focused on the things they had in common rather than differences. Could that work in Richmond too? Could focusing on commonalities among denominations be the key to reconciling differences?

Again, I was in over my head, but fearlessly and excitedly shared my vision with the church board members. After their approval, I contacted the key religious leaders in Richmond and persuaded them to join me in creating an ecumenical meeting around Pentecost. We called the meeting Pentecost '79 and Reverend Dr. James Forbes spoke to three thousand people in attendance. Everyone put aside their denominational differences, their gender differences, their racial differences, even their generational differences. For a few hours one Saturday night in 1979, the people of God gathered under one roof in Richmond, Virginia and worshiped the One who plants and the One who harvests. We never felt so rooted.

41
LEADING

"Slow down, Preacher!"

WEAG had grown to be influential in Richmond. Pentecost '79 stirred our city to think about each other as brothers and sisters in Christ and nurtured a positive atmosphere among the whole Church in RVA. We encouraged each other in our faith and WEAG earned a clear place of leadership in the city as a loving and inclusive church community. I was asked to speak at leadership retreats and share the story of WEAG. Pastors wanted to hear how WEAG impacted our city as well as supported missions in other countries. These speaking opportunities challenged me to identify specific leadership principles through personal reading and study. *Spiritual Leadership*, by J. Oswald Sanders, was a favorite, along with articles from the magazines *Christianity Today* and *Leadership*. I pored over passages in the Bible and closely observed the lives of Moses, Paul, and of course, Jesus. Their leadership styles created solid templates for shepherding, serving, and teaching.

I knew leaders needed a support network so I typically attended a monthly gathering with other ministers in our denomination. The gathering required a full day commitment with a two hour drive one way, meetings, dinner, and an evening service. However, I believed that pastors needed the support of other pastors. As WEAG grew, the demands on my time and energy grew as well. One morning I sat in my study on the day of the ministers' gathering, wrestling with whether or not to attend. I felt like the Lord was urging me to go to the meeting and think about serving others. He also made it clear that I should pay attention to my own personal growth and he would take care of the future. I got in my car and drove to the meeting.

As I walked in they were singing, "I am free from the fear of tomorrow, I am free from the guilt of the past....I have traded my sorrows for a heavenly crown....I'm free praise the Lord I'm free at last." Something shifted inside me. God used that song to touch my heart and shape my decisions about serving my network and tending to my own personal growth. An ordained connection to this network of pastors settled in and balanced the constant pulls on pastoral life ... spiritual pride, misplaced focus, juggling priorities, functioning as an independent rather than a part of something. I needed this group of ministers and they needed me.

With four services each Sunday and renting two other buildings to accommodate all the space we needed for ministry, it was time for WEAG to expand in space and staff. Years ago I had observed a brother and brother-in-law on staff together at Bethel Assembly of God, where Ira Stanphill and John Wilkerson pastored together. So hiring my brother-in-law, John Hershman, fresh out of seminary made sense. I knew I could trust him.

We began construction on an activities building to provide a small gym, increased worship space and more classrooms, but this quickly grew into a nightmare. We overspent on a poorly constructed building and fell into mounting debt and unpaid bills. People sat in pews angry about the debt and all they had sacrificially given. Other issues were festering as well. The Faith Movement, an offshoot of the Charismatic Movement, was picking up speed and making theological waves in the congregation. A group of church members grew unhappy with WEAG's leadership and accused us of not having "enough faith." They believed if someone had enough faith there would be no debt, no sickness, no struggles. Where were the healings? Where was the prosperity? Where were the blessings? These questions stirred doubt and confusion among the congregation.

Another stressor during this time was the shift WEAG made in leadership style. Originally WEAG's constitution supported a Pastor/Deacon Board model, but recently had been changed to a Pastor/Elder/Deacon model. The introduction of Elders and the level of their influence and authority in the church was an issue for a small group of people. The final straw was a bold, orange wall that the architect insisted was the right color for the sanctuary backdrop. It seemed to aggravate rather than comfort or inspire the congregation. How was I supposed to lead an angry flock? How were we going to pay back the hundreds of thousands we owed? None of my training had prepared me for this rabbit hole.

It was stress that eventually sent me to the ER with chest pains one evening. I was sure I was having a heart attack. "Slow down, Preacher," were the doctor's parting words when he discharged me. Anxiety was my diagnosis. How was I supposed to slow down? Which problem needed less of my attention?

John Hershman, my brother-in-law, stood in the doorway of my office one morning and proposed an impossible, yet intriguing idea.

"Bob, we need to focus on missions and build a church for someone else who is in greater need than we are."

Maybe John was right. Maybe looking outward and giving generously at a time when we were struggling mightily was a prophetic word, even though it seemed like the most upside-down, backwards way of dealing with the problems at hand. A widow offering her last two mites at the temple, a young boy on a hillside in Galilee offering the only food he had for the day, Elijah asking a young woman and her starving child to make a cake for him out of their last bit of oil and flour ... these images played in my mind like a movie as I pondered John's words. I preached on these stories.

I had read them in the Bible more times than I could count. I truly believed there was no way to out give God. But did I believe enough for a whole congregation? More importantly, did WEAG trust the pastoral leadership enough to embrace a bold move like this?

It was a challenging time in the life of WEAG. Some people left angry. Most stayed, but some grumbled and criticized, creating an unsettling environment. I did the only thing I knew how to do well. I prayed. I prayed like I had never prayed before. I also fell apart a little bit. One afternoon my secretary called Joan and said, "I think you should come to the office. Bob's having a rough time." Joan came and sat with me as I crumbled under the heavy weight of leadership in dark times. She sat with me and comforted me and listened. We prayed together and agreed that circumstances looked dire, but God was still in control. I took a few days off to manage my stress and gain perspective.

Three things got us through the fire. We shared John's vision of a mission trip with the congregation and amazingly raised $20,000.00 to build two churches in the Dominican Republic. People from WEAG volunteered to travel to an extremely poor country and harsh conditions for two weeks to help another community in need. This unassuming project opened the door for God to start meeting our own need. Missions had always been a major focus, but John's leadership elevated it with hands-on opportunities. Within two years we paid off the money we owed in construction debt.

Secondly, our leadership decided we were a church, not a convention center. With the emergence of the Charismatic Renewal and WEAG's influence in Richmond, people flocked to attend on Sunday mornings, but only a small number served and intentionally embraced being a part of the church community. We maintained vibrant worship, but began to focus deeply on discipleship and encouraged people to become more involved through missions, adult education classes, and eventually a fine arts program that grew over time. The staff also agreed that our response to the Faith Movement issue was not to argue and blame, but to redirect and educate the congregation around what the Bible said about faith. Through sermons and adult Sunday School classes we began to teach and disciple. We lost some members to the Faith Movement, but WEAG gained understanding and a deeper faith through studying scripture together and praying for wisdom.

Finally, we repainted the wall. Instead of an irritating orange as the focal point, a calming beige greeted the congregation. People began smiling in church again. There was an atmosphere of expectancy rather than evaluation. I stopped focusing on how much we owed and who might be leaving next. I discovered that when you shift the focus to strengthening the body of Christ, wounds heal, debts shrink, and people grow.

Leading requires staying, not quitting. Sometimes it requires courage, like giving generously out of scarcity. Other times it requires humility, like listening to other leaders around you. Occasionally it's as simple as changing the color of a wall. Mostly, though, it's a combination: stay, be courageous, practice humility, and never underestimate the power of a simple solution.

42
SEEING

"Eyes that look are common; eyes that see are rare."
J. Oswald Sanders

I started working on a Doctor of Ministry degree at Union
Theological Seminary in Richmond around the same time we started
building more space for WEAG. I had no way of knowing the
stressful season that lay ahead, but I had always dreamed of pursuing
more education after my time at Wheaton. Learning energized
me and even though it added another ball into my juggling act, it
provided a healthy distraction. Shortly after I hired John, we agreed
to hire one more pastor to help cover WEAG's rapid growth. Bill
Martin was a perfect fit. With John Hershman on staff covering
missions, college, and young adults, and Bill Martin, overseeing
education, youth and family, I finally had support in place to handle
extra church responsibilities while I was in class. Without their hard
work, generous spirit, and dedication to WEAG, I could never have
pursued higher education.

My project for the degree was on racial reconciliation in the
church. I studied the history of black and white congregations
in Richmond, as well as relationships between black and white
churches. One of the classes I took was offered at Virginia Union
Seminary, a black university in close proximity to Union Theological
Seminary. The class, Contemporary Theology, was taught in a

seminar style with only ten to twelve students participating. I was the only white person. One day as we were talking about inequities in our culture particularly related to the way black people were treated by white people and how the church had failed to lead by example in reconciliation, the conversation grew very denigrating toward the white community. Comments even seemed to justify the attitude that the black community had toward the white community. I remained silent and just listened. The professor eventually looked at me and said, "So what are you thinking Mr. Rhoden?"

"May I tell you my story?" I asked.

"Go ahead," he said.

"When I was two, a black man who was driving recklessly, possibly even intoxicated, killed my mom and step-dad as they walked along the highway one evening. I was an only child and my grandmother raised me until I was 12. After that I moved in with other relatives, but never completely felt like I belonged. I grew up in a very prejudiced community in northern Florida, but I've worked hard to shed old prejudices. I believe that in Christ there is no room for negative attitudes toward anyone based on skin color. In Christ, even when my flesh tries to convince me that I have every right to judge a group of people because of what happened to my parents, I am still called to treat all people with respect and dignity."

When I finished there was an awkward silence in the room. The professor thanked me for sharing and we moved on. Toward the end of class one of the students seated next to me discreetly passed a note that read, "Don't judge all of us by what you have heard in class today." We exchanged a smile ... a symbol of hope for both of us. That afternoon we all started the class with "common eyes that look", according to J. Oswald Sanders, but by the end of class, some of us left with "rare eyes that see."

As a culmination of my work, I organized two worship services where WEAG and Great Hope Baptist, a black congregation in Richmond, worshipped together. For the first service, WEAG's congregation visited Great Hope on a Sunday evening for the service. The second time, Great Hope's pastor preached at WEAG on a Sunday evening and along with some of his congregation we worshipped together. I wanted the experience to help us develop eyes to "see" rather than "look." I understood reconciliation in my head, but my heart needed to understand too. In the light of Christ, worshipping alongside people who had been misunderstood, mistreated, and misrepresented because of the color of their skin gave all of us a way to "see" each other.

There were other ways I began to "see" rather than "look" during this busy time in the middle of my life. I realized I needed to intentionally carve out time for my wife and children. I needed to enjoy being present with them. Mrs. Robins gave our family a gift of membership to the Jewish Community Center in town, so we started making Friday nights family night. We spent time together and swam in the indoor pool at the center or enjoyed activities in the center's gym. I taught all three kids to swim. "Reach, pull, and kick," I encouraged as my hands supported their small frames in the water. I gave them countless rides on my back across the pool until our skin grew waterlogged and raisined.

I volunteered to keep score at my son's baseball games. Joan and I stole occasional dates when we could afford a babysitter, and we took a family vacation every summer. We didn't have a lot of extra money, but were fortunate to have several members in our congregation who generously offered us the use of their vacation homes. My kids still talk about the fun we had on those vacations. Even the rainy ones where we played way too much Yahtzee and Old Maid. Spending quality time together allowed us to truly "see" each other.

We visited Aunt Inez and Uncle E.D. most summers and tried to attend the family reunion so I could see other aunts, uncles, and cousins. They all wanted to see my family and hear about our life in Virginia. I was one of the few in the family who left Florida and started a whole new path on my own. My kids knew about Granny Cobb and had seen pictures of my mom, Martha Lee. They eventually found out about Harold Rhoden and Drew Stickland. My own story had settled deep in my bones by now, but every once in a while it still ached when I thought about it. Why did Drew leave before I was born? Why didn't he ever come back to see me? Had he ever thought about me? Did I look like him? Even though he had died, my mind sometimes worked to iron out these questions like wrinkles in a shirt. I always loved seeing my relatives, but the visits stirred conflicting emotions inside like gain and loss, joy and pain, acceptance and loneliness.

On Mother's Day and Father's Day I often referenced my story during a sermon at WEAG. I shared about my mom and stepdad being killed, living with Granny Cobb, and meeting Harold in the hospital. I shared how I found out Harold wasn't my biological father and how Drew Strickland entered my story. I weaved these stories together or focused on the thought that we don't all have answers to our pasts. I often ended by telling the church they were my extended family. God had surrounded a small, forlorn Baker County boy with more family than patches on a quilt. I "looked" at my WEAG family every Sunday, but when I shared my story with them, I was finally able to "see" them as family.

43
SHARING

"Bob if I had any idea this church was going to grow to this size I would have given you more land!"

I sat in the parlor with Julia Robins. Over the years we had developed a friendship, and I stopped by occasionally to visit and give updates on the church. She also took an interest in my family and loved having us visit her at "Raleigh" during the holidays. WEAG was growing again. Our staff now included a music and fine arts minister, Bob Laughlin, from the Atlanta area. Anything he envisioned, directed, organized, or nurtured grew by leaps and bounds. He had the midas touch when it came to fostering a creative worship experience. WEAG started gaining a reputation not only for missions and outreach, but for engaging worship and musical productions centered around the life of Christ. These productions drew crowds of more than 20,000 at Easter and Christmas. One Wednesday evening at the weekly Bible study I asked how many people started attending WEAG because of a music and fine arts production? Over 250 people raised their hands.

More people equaled more cars. More cars meant more parking spaces. More parking spaces created a dilemma. One Sunday the ushers reported 46 cars parked along Parham road during the 11 am service. Parham road was two lanes and scheduled to become four lanes very soon. We knew there would be no roadside parking allowed on a four lane road. As I discussed this new problem with Mrs. Robins she shook her head and said, "If I had any idea this church was going to grow to this size I would have given you more land!" She agreed to help us locate new property to build a new facility and provide more parking.

Within a few months she had arranged for us to purchase land less than a mile from our current location on Parham road. She generously gave us $100,000 toward the purchase, and this excited the congregation so much that we raised the remainder in a very short time. However, because of the stress of our last building project, no one was eager to rush into this. The church leadership and the congregation agreed to hold off on the relocation project until we paid for the land and secured the right architect and construction company. We also needed to sell our current facility. Who in the world wanted to buy a church building?

In the process of looking for land to relocate we had originally approached a Jewish congregation about selling the 15 acres of undeveloped land they owned right next to us. They were uninterested. Our leadership and congregation committed to pray and fast for God to provide the land another way, and he did through Mrs. Robin's generosity; but we still had to sell. One morning the president of a newly formed Jewish congregation in town called me and asked to meet. We met for lunch at a local restaurant and after some polite small talk, he leaned across the table and said, "Let me get to the point. We are interested in buying your property."

I tried to hide my excitement and listened intently as he explained their need for a building and a place to grow. I nodded and empathized with the many decisions a leader faces when caring for a congregation. By the time our plates were cleared and our glasses held the remnants of watered down sweet tea, we were talking like it was a done deal. Within a few weeks, the president of a Jewish congregation and a pentecostal preacher sat in the little chapel, surrounded by triangled windows of hope, and struck a deal for WEAG's asking price. We agreed to let them occupy space immediately and share the facility during our building process. The verbal agreement was officially approved by our respective congregations and all the necessary legal paperwork created and properly executed.

For the next two years a Jewish congregation and a Christian congregation shared space. Because our meeting times were different and they only used the chapel, it was an easy arrangement. There was one issue we had to work out beforehand. A cross, which was problematic for a Jewish congregation, sat on the roof of our chapel. They could not consecrate the building for their use with a cross on the outside. Would we consider removing the cross? We agreed to consider it, but wondered how that would look if we removed such a significant symbol of our faith.

As our whole congregation, from adult to child, talked through this difficult decision we explored and discussed the idea that our faith is not contained in a symbol alone, although the symbol remains very important to us. What if removing the cross created a way for both congregations to worship and actually increased our faith? Maybe the chapel's shared space could become a sign of cooperation between faiths? We agreed to take the cross down from the top of our chapel building and move it to our new building as a reminder of how God provided for us. On the day the cross came down representatives from both congregations were present. We embraced each other as friends and they thanked us for being sensitive to their request and not viewing it as anti-Christian, but a gesture of love and concern for them.

The large metal ring of our "tongues of fire" remained hanging in the chapel. For us it was a reminder of the Holy Spirit, God's gift of power and comfort to his people. The Jewish congregation called it the "burning bush" and for them it was a reminder of Holiness,

God's presence and voice to his people. We shared the "tongues of fire" and "burning bush" for two years in the chapel's sacred space of hope. For a short time in the mid-80's on the West End of Richmond, Jew and Gentile shared space. Space for understanding. Space for friendship. Space for worshipping a God who sees our hearts, knows our minds, and loves us more than we could ever deserve.

44
ACCESS

If you receive the white dot, you'll know you have access."

I stared at my friend, Jim Linen. On the outside I wore my cool, collected expression while he explained the white dot experience to me, but inside my heart raced with excitement and my thoughts cartwheeled around my brain.

"Right before the photo session starts, whoever is granted access to the president will receive a small white dot pressed to their coat lapel. If you receive the white dot, you'll know you have access."

Why in the world would anyone give me access to a photo session with President Ronald Reagan? How did I end up here? What would I say if I met the President?

Jim Linen, a high profile media executive and businessman, moved from Florida to Richmond, Virginia in the early 80's. and ended up attending a WEAG men's prayer meeting because a pastor in Florida recommended it. Jim shared his story of business and personal life challenges with the men, and he also shared a promise he made to God; if God saved his company from bankruptcy, he would give back generously. Despite the theological feathers Jim's barter may have ruffled, I was intrigued. Jim had charisma and confidence and interesting perspectives, but he also had a vulnerable side he showed at the prayer meeting that evening. One could hardly blame him for bargaining with God. In fact, bargaining with God was practically biblical, at least in the Old Testament. Abraham, Moses, Gideon - these men conversed, debated, and bargained with God regularly. Maybe this was the path Jim needed to walk to find a meaningful relationship with Christ.

The company pulled out of possible bankruptcy and Jim kept his promise to God. He continued attending WEAG and asked me to be one of three trustees for a charitable trust he set up to help individuals or organizations who were in ministry, but struggling. "Miracle money," he called it. Jim stayed through WEAG's transition from 501 Parham Road to our new location a half mile down the road. He stayed despite what the Bible has to say about wealth and how hard it is for a rich man to enter the gates of heaven. Jim Linen was hungry for a relationship with Christ and generously shared his resources with WEAG whether through financial gifts or connecting us with his vast array of contacts. His genuine desire to make a difference for Christ and his Kingdom grew way past the simple bargain he made with God.

We became friends and enjoyed each other's company. When he invited me to join him at a White House function and said I might have the chance to meet the president, Ronald Reagan, and have a picture taken with him, I said "yes" before Jim could finish the sentence. I was fortunate enough to receive a white dot on my lapel that special evening, shake hands with Ronald Reagan, and have my picture taken with him. It was an unbelievable day and one I knew I would never forget. What I didn't realize was how short my friendship with Jim would turn out to be.

Two years later Jim and his wife, Diane, were in London for Wimbledon when Jim attempted to cross the street and looked the wrong way as he stepped off a curb. It was a common mistake to make while visiting another country, but a costly one, as a van approached and the driver, having no time to brake, hit him. Luminaries like Billy Graham came to pray for Jim, who hovered between life and death in a London hospital for four days before taking his last breath at the young age of 51. The whole church was in shock with the news of Jim's death.

Diane planned a public memorial service to be held in WEAG's new sanctuary followed by a small family graveside funeral held in Pennsylvania a few days later. She asked me to preside over both services. I felt completely overwhelmed with grief, as well as fully responsible to present Jim's life in a way that honored Christ without offending all the media moguls and northeastern politicians that planned to attend. The memorial service went well and many business executives came up afterward and expressed appreciation for the meaningful tribute to Jim.

Jim's family flew me to Scranton, Pennsylvania with my son, Rob, who was studying to become a minister at the time. We stayed at the home of Jim's uncle, Governor Scranton, who had been governor of Pennsylvania, a presidential candidate, and an ambassador to the UN under President Nixon. Rob and I listened to Governor Scranton tell story after story the night we flew in and were captivated by all he had experienced in his political career. Jim and I were polar opposites when it came to how we were raised. I was from rice and gravy, a one-room school, and Granny. Jim was from salad forks, private school, and political status. Still, we both needed Jesus. He was our Savior and our access to God. Regardless of what we had or didn't have in this life, our need for a Savior was the common denominator.

As I lay in bed that evening an idea came to me for the small service the next day. In the morning, I gathered some supplies and shared the idea with Rob. When it was time for me to speak at the graveside service I told the story of Jim inviting me to meet President Ronald Reagan and the power of the white dot. As I spoke about Jim leaving us, I took a small white dot I had cut out earlier and pressed it on top of the casket as a symbol of Jim's faith in Jesus granting him access to the King of Kings! It was one of those moments that moved me, the minister, as much as the people listening.

Access into Jim's world gave me clear vision and verified a truth I already knew; all of us need a Savior. In the next decade I would have many more opportunities to rub shoulders with politicians and businessmen; but no one was ever too big or too small, too rich or too poor, too strong or too weak for God to save. Believing that Jesus, the Son of God, took all the sin of the world and forgave it by dying on a cross and resurrecting after three days so we might live - that belief is the only white dot that would ever really matter. Life after death. No more pain. Eternal joy. Who wouldn't want access to that?

45
FAREWELL

"In his heart a man plans his course,
but the Lord determines his steps".
Proverbs 16:9

When I began my personal faith journey at Lantana Community Church in November, 1958 I wanted to be a missionary. At Toccoa Falls Bible College this desire strengthened with the strong emphasis on missions. When Teen Challenge came into the picture my desire evolved into being a missionary evangelist. With my next season of ministry starting in 1969 as a pastor, I realized I may have plans, but the Lord was definitely "determining my steps." I never really thought I would be a pastor. As a matter of fact when we started WEAG, Joan and I had a five year plan and thought we would move to the mission field after that, but God had a different course prepared.

During my years at WEAG I grew and learned a lot about shepherding a group of people and daily listening to the voice of the Holy Spirit. The church had regular ups and downs that impacted the congregation: attendance fluctuated, sometimes expenses exceeded offerings, negative opinions occasionally swayed morale, and there were always seasons of intense personal need for different families and individuals. Raising my own family and maintaining a healthy marriage required effort, time, prayer, faith. Just trying to be present at home when my mind might be somewhere else took energy. In a blink our toddlers turned into grade-schoolers and navigated their way through our neighborhood elementary school; then entered the awkward years of middle school, and finally high school.

No one gets through life without pain and troubles. Our family was no exception. Our youngest daughter, Cindy, was attacked by a neighbor's dog when she was five, and the initial damage to her face was so extensive the doctor thought she would need plastic surgery later. The healing was long, but the scarring was minimal and in the end, she never needed surgery. Our oldest daughter, Julie, had constant abdominal pain in high school and lost so much weight we grew extremely concerned. It wasn't until college that she was diagnosed with Crohns disease and our family learned how to support her in dealing with a chronic illness. There was always that balancing act of parenting teens: when to step in and when to hold back. Joan and I didn't always get it right.

Through all the years of shepherding my own family and a church family, I also became more and more involved with leadership in the Assemblies of God at the district level. I became a presbyter or director over the Southern Potomac District and oversaw about twenty-five ministers and their congregations. I acted as a resource and first line of contact for these churches, led monthly fellowship meetings for ministers, and attended quarterly meetings for presbyters. Eventually, I became an executive presbyter with more responsibility. Years before, when I had begrudgingly yet obediently sacrificed an entire day each month to connect with other pastors in my area, I wondered if it was worth the hassle. Obedience and time are subtle, trustworthy pavers that frequently create paths and roads to new opportunities.

Over time I began to receive invitations to speak to other pastors at conferences and to lead church leadership retreats. Concurrently, I was rising to new levels of leadership in the Assemblies of God

Potomac District which included Virginia, Maryland, West Virginia, and Washington DC. As the District Superintendent, our "bishop" for the area, approached retirement, conversation started circulating that I was well-suited to serve in that role. It was flattering, but I couldn't imagine being chosen for a leadership position of that caliber.

WEAG was settled into the new building and thriving in the new space. It was hard to believe we actually had adequate space for worship, education, offices, and parking. As we transitioned into the new space and developed some new ways to minister, I had so much happening inside my heart. I was tired and needed time to think, so I took mini sabbaticals in the summer months for the next few years. Julie, a recent college grad, was getting married in the summer of '91. Rob was three years into college and Cindy had just started college. Joan was teaching again to help with all the added expenses. Our family was changing and I sensed change was coming to WEAG too. But what kind of change? What was God asking of me? On Easter of '91 we reached an attendance of 2000. God was still moving in this place. Why was I preparing for potential change? I had other job offers and opportunities over the years, but this felt different. I recognized the restlessness in my heart and knew I couldn't ignore it.

By May of '91 the unexpected happened. I was elected to serve as the new District Superintendent of the Potomac District. The district's headquarters was in Fairfax, Virginia, a couple of hours from Richmond. The job was a huge responsibility and accepting it meant moving to Fairfax, Virginia and leaving a church body I dearly loved. My time at WEAG was coming to a close. In June I walked Julie down the aisle and said a farewell of sorts to being the main male influence in her life. In July, I preached my final sermon as the pastor of WEAG with a lump in my throat and tears running down my face. Farewells are never easy.

The farewell I remember most vividly happened on a Thursday night toward the end of July. I had an exit plan. The Lord put an idea in my heart to walk through the church building and say a final farewell by myself. It was about 11 pm that night when I started journeying through every room, every hallway, and under the tongues of fire. Finally, I stood quietly in the familiar position behind the pulpit. As I wrapped my hands around the sides of the pulpit, handmade by a craftsman in the congregation, I thought of all the Sundays I had stood in that very spot and preached scores of sermons. I stared out at the quiet, dark sanctuary and waited for the tears to come, but they didn't. Why couldn't I cry now on my last night in the building, when just four days ago I wept through the whole sermon?

You can't cry because the people aren't here. You can't weep for the building. It's the people you weep for.

The thought was so clear it almost felt as though it was spoken out loud. I nodded and said quietly, "I get it, Lord." I made my way back to the office, left my keys on the desk, walked out of the church building, and stepped into a whole new season determined by God.

46
STIR

"Now who's responsible for this warm welcome?"

I opened the middle drawer of my desk and discovered a set of handcuffs on my first official day in the district office as Superintendent. I threw my head back and laughed; then walked the hallways holding them up and asking people about them. I thought it was a joke. There were a few polite smiles and finally someone told me the story behind the cuffs. They had been in the drawer for decades because one of my predecessors enjoyed serving as the night watchman at a church camp in West Virginia. He patrolled for the campers' safety and clipped these handcuffs on his belt just in case he ever encountered an intruder. He wanted to be prepared for anything. After his terms as superintendent, he stepped down, but the handcuffs stayed. I had fun showing them to some of my close friends for a few months before I discarded them for good. My goal was to create a whole new culture in the Potomac District.

When I accepted the position as District Superintendent of the Potomac District, Joan and I knew we would need to move since the office was located in Fairfax, Virginia, a couple hours north of Richmond. We were officially empty nesters. With our oldest married and living in Illinois, and our other two in college out of state, there was no reason to stay in Richmond. However, we had lived there for 22 years and established relationships in the community. Some of

Joan's family still lived in Richmond and our whole life was there … doctors, dentist, hair stylists, familiar grocery stores, neighbors, friends, a tightly-knit church community. Moving would not only be a major physical change for us, but an emotional one as well. After many tearful conversations about how we would walk into this new season, we agreed to approach the first year of my position as a series of adjustments and not jump in all at once.

Joan needed time to say goodbye to Richmond and ready the house to sell. I wanted to take time to find a house in Northern Virginia that suited us and could comfortably hold our expanding family on holidays, as well as become a place to invite pastors and their families for meals. This meant Joan and I were apart during most of the week, and I logged a lot of hours commuting back and forth.

The perceived culture of the Potomac District tended to be extremely conservative, yet WEAG was a forward thinking, creative church. How would I handle the challenge of this dichotomy? My new role loomed before me, and I wondered where to begin. There was no real job description for the District Superintendent and this lack of direction was both exciting and nerve-wracking. One night I decided to do what I typically do when I need to think; I took a drive.

I picked the Washington D.C. beltway as my think tank and made the 64 mile loop twice as I shared my heart with God. I spoke. I sang. I asked questions. Had I made the right decision coming to Fairfax? Could I be comfortable with being uncomfortable in this new challenge? You could say I was plugged into God's GPS. It's amazing how God can transform a busy multi-lane highway into sacred space. After a while I grew quiet and just listened. It was barely a whisper, but the words were clear and assured the depths of my heart.

I will be with you and guide you. Trust me and see what I will do.

I crawled into bed in my hotel room at 2 a.m. after three or four hours of circling the beltway. I fell sound asleep knowing two things.

I was in the right place; and I was definitely going to need fuel for the car in the morning.

After a year of commuting and adjusting to a new leadership role, Joan and I bid farewell to Richmond and moved to Fairfax. One of the positive things about moving was that our good friends, Dick and Ruth Foth, had also recently moved to the same area. We knew the Foths from my grad school days at Wheaton and were excited to live so close again and rekindle our friendship. While Dick and I figured out ways to connect some of our work, Joan and Ruth spent hours poring through thrift shops and antique malls. They took walks and swapped books, and most likely compared stories about their husbands and all the ways we drove them crazy! They fed each other's souls and commiserated about being away from family and living outside of their comfort zones. The four of us shared many meals together and enjoyed reminiscing about our grad school days.

Dick served with the International Fellowship which helped facilitate things like the National Prayer Breakfast and supported congressmen, senators, ambassadors, and other political figures. He and I both believed in the power of mentoring, so we set up a mentoring opportunity for younger ministers in the Potomac District. Over a period of four years we mentored forty younger ministers, Mark Batterson being one of them. The work was exciting and created a stir among young ministers in the area. Mentoring became a unique part of the Potomac District's DNA.

Occasionally, Dick invited pastors from around the country to come for three days and experience how God was working in the halls of government in D.C. Many government leaders and politicians flew under the radar, but others were very open with their faith. Because of my role as a religious leader in the Washington, D.C. area and my friendship with Dick Foth, I was invited to a special prayer breakfast in response to the horrific burning of several black churches in the South. President Clinton rallied spiritual leaders from across the nation and asked us to join together and use our influence to stop this tragic, racist activity.

When the announcement, "Ladies and Gentlemen, please welcome the President of the United States," fell on a hushed room, the words seemed to trumpet into the air like bright notes in a patriotic overture. I was seated at a round table for eight in the Abraham Lincoln room. There was only one seat left at our table and I started wondering if that seat might be for President Clinton. I told myself that was just wishful thinking. When President Clinton walked up to my table and sat down, I took a deep breath and tried to remind myself that he was just a regular guy who brushed his teeth with a regular toothbrush and blew his nose into regular tissue. However, being in the presence of an authority figure like the President of the United States stirred an adrenaline rush I couldn't deny.

The room was filled with big names. Next to the President was Jack Kemp, a former professional football player, former member of the House of Representatives, and contender for the presidential nomination in the 1988 Republican primaries. Other tables included notables like Jesse Jackson, and Dr. Don Argue, President of the National Association of Evangelicals. There was a heavy cloud of somber reflection as we were all still processing the sickening news of these churches and people who had been persecuted for no other reason than the color of their skin. Our conversations focused on how spiritual leaders around the country could work to prevent hateful acts like this. At the end of the breakfast, I was asked to give the benediction. It was an honor I will never forget and reminded me of that white dot I acquired with my friend, Jim Linen, a few years before.

I stood up and petitioned God to give us wisdom and courage and guidance as we worked to bring healing and reconciliation to our nation. As I left the prayer breakfast, I felt excited and anticipatory. I assumed it was from spending the morning with the President, but maybe I sensed another shift, another change coming. Little did I know that as a new chapter in my story was being written, an old chapter was starting to stir.

47
WAVES

Dear Bobby,
I have some news to share with you...

One ordinary day in September, 1994, I received a short letter from Aunt Inez. She shared the news that Harold Rhoden had died. I didn't attend his funeral, but the event pulled at me, creating an ebb and flow of reflection much like the moon's gravitational pull generates an ocean's tide. I had a picture of Harold Rhoden, the man who gave me a name. I had a picture of Ashley Weeks, the man who gave me a future. But I did not have a picture of Drew Strickland, the man who gave me life.

At the age of 52, my days were still busy, but my restless heart felt more settled. I had carved out a life filled with family and ministry and purpose. I didn't need to find answers to old questions, but as I reflected on my life I realized that if there were answers, I'd like to know. Joan and I decided to drive to Florida and search for my father's family. Maybe I could at least find a picture of the man who gave me life. A new adventure awaited us.

My cousin Angie had been very close to my mom and shared many stories with me over the years. So when I called and explained to her I was interested in finding a photograph of my biological father, she agreed to help me find information and connect with his relatives for a picture. She knew that my dad had a brother named Covey, and she thought he might still be living in Jacksonville, Florida. We searched genealogical records and visited a few cemeteries where some of my dad's family was buried to see if Covey was still living. I asked questions in the little town of Olustee. Did anyone know Covey Strickland? Where did he live? Eventually enough digging and conversations and phone calls led us to Covey.

On a Friday night in October, I cautiously dialed a number and waited through a few rings to see who might answer. My heart raced a little faster and my mouth felt dry as a family member answered the phone and said Covey was not available, but they would have him return the call. I waited and paced anxiously. Would he call me back? What if he didn't get the message? Or what if he just ignored it? My mind volleyed these thoughts back and forth like a ball bouncing between two ping pong paddles. I had put something into motion and now all I could do was wait.

Two hours later the phone rang. I had rehearsed this conversation a thousand times in my head, but I could never have imagined the response when I explained who I was and how I was looking for a picture of my dad. There was a pause and then Covey said, "I know about you!" Four words of confirmation that changed my life. I … know … about … you.

The next day, Joan and I drove to Uncle Covey's apartment on the southside of Jacksonville. A short, stocky man with grey cropped hair answered the door. He smiled and invited us in.

We chatted for almost an hour going over all the information I had, and then he filled in the gaps. His brother, Drew, had been a hired farm hand for my Granny. He and my mom liked each other, but once he realized she was pregnant, Drew left and never looked back. I listened to Covey tell the story and thought about how such a short-lived fling could send ripples through so many lives. "Your dad died when he was 30 from a heart damaged by rheumatic fever when he was young. But did you know your dad married and had three daughters? I stay in touch with the girls and I think they would want to know they have an older brother they've never met."

Nervously I explained that I wasn't there to make waves in anyone's family. I just wanted a picture of my dad. Covey reached in a stack of pictures and handed me an old photo of a young man, maybe around 19 or 20. It was like looking in a mirror. We had the same eyes, the same mouth, the same freckled skin.

"Your sisters' names are Hester, Allene, and Sharon. I'm gonna tell the girls about you and see what they think."

I nodded quietly and marveled at how complete I felt. Somebody knew about me. I looked like my dad. I had sisters; real flesh and blood sisters.

That night I lay in bed and replayed everything in my head. I have sisters! I said it out loud several times just to make sure I wasn't dreaming. Emotions rolled over me like waves coming in with the tide - rising, cresting, breaking, crashing - a rhythm so ancient and natural, yet so wild. I couldn't calm the sea, so I just let it wash over me. I was about to explore the depths of a carefully guarded secret and all its ripples. My story's truest narrative was within reach.

48
REJOICE

"Rejoice with your family in the beautiful land of life."
Albert Einstein

After I told my children (and anyone else who would listen) that I saw a picture of my dad and discovered I have three sisters, there was nothing to do but travel home and wait. I tried to resume my regular duties as District Superintendent - helping pastors and churches with transitions, planning the annual ministers retreat, overseeing weekly staff meetings, preaching in a different church each Sunday, and a host of other responsibilities - but I was distracted with this new, exciting family information. What was going to happen next? Would I ever get to talk to my sisters or even meet them? Did they look like me? Did they talk like me? What if they were wonderful people? What if they weren't? These questions circled my brain, like planes waiting for a signal to land.

About a week later Uncle Covey called and said the girls wanted to talk to me and possibly meet. He gave me Allene's number and said I should call her. How do you begin a conversation with a sister you've never met? Should I offer to fly down to Florida and meet them? Should Joan go with me? What did they think about preachers? Nervously, I dialed the number. Allene answered with a "hello," and I simply said, "Hi Allene, this is Bob." Watching my own daughters interact and chat for hours about anything and everything,

I should not have been surprised by how easily the conversation flowed. Allene, my amazing sister, was easy and comfortable, warm and friendly, carefree and funny, carrying a conversation no matter the situation. Her first words were, "This is amazing! We have an older brother."

She asked me to tell a little bit about myself and the story I knew that connected us. Eventually, after she was convinced I wasn't some crazy person trying to weasel my way into the family, she suggested I fly down to Florida and meet her and my youngest sister, Sharon, who lived close to Allene. Hester, the oldest of the three sisters, lived in Pennsylvania. I agreed to call her and make arrangements to meet sometime when I was traveling in the northeast.

I hung up the phone and spent the next hour talking about everything to Joan. It was hard to put into words how I was feeling. Everything I knew about being a brother I had learned from living with my cousins in Jacksonville as a teenager, observing the adult relationship between Joan and her brother, John, and watching my son, Rob, relate to his sisters. Learning to be a sibling as an adult felt like pulling an all-nighter cramming for an exam the next day. Being the oldest of the siblings and the only male felt even trickier.

When I flew to Orlando alone in early January, I rented a car and drove to Vero Beach. As I pulled into the driveway I watched Allene walk out of her house and toward me. I stepped out of the car tentatively, but she ignored that completely and threw her arms around me.

"Welcome," she said grinning from ear to ear. She had the friendliest grin I had ever seen!

With that, the ice was broken. Her husband, Tom, and the dog were waiting inside. Allene noticed that I tensed up as soon as I saw the dog, but she assured me he was a friendly German Shepherd. I hoped so! I pushed through my fear and made small talk with Tom and Allene as we waited for my youngest sister, Sharon, and her husband, Buz, to arrive. Soon we were all five under one roof. Sharon and Buz were more reserved than Allene and Tom, but everyone was friendly and curious about each other.

Over a lasagna dinner in Allene and Tom's dining room, I shared my childhood story and how I found Covey 50 years later. I explained that I visited Covey recently hoping for a picture of my biological dad and some sense of who he was as a person, but discovered a whole lot more. Everyone was intrigued with my story and how it connected to theirs. Then Allene jumped in.

"Bob, when Covey, called me and told me about you, I said, 'Covey, what are you talking about?' Then I put my hand over the phone and hoarsely whispered to the rest of the family, 'Hey, ya'll, this is Covey and he says we have a brother!'"

We all laughed at Allene's animated retelling. She and Sharon told me that they had little to no memory of Drew as their father because Allene was only two when he died, and Sharon, born a month after his death. Their mom had remarried and their stepdad was who they thought of as their father. He had also passed away, but their mom was still living and battling Alztheimers. Both of my sisters said that I had helped them understand a little more about Drew. Their mom hadn't spoken of him much. It was all a lot to take in, but I was glad I had come to visit.

As the evening uncurled, everyone grew more comfortable and Allene and Sharon both encouraged me to visit Hester sometime soon. It was late when we hugged good-bye and promised to keep in touch. I drove back to my hotel feeling content, complete, and connected. Connected not just by experience or relationship, but by an irrefutable sense of belonging, as if orchestrated by divine appointment. After years and years of wondering, I had found my people. I rejoiced in the unexpected beauty of it all, and it seemed that every chirping cricket, every croaking frog, every buzzing cicada in the Florida night symphony rejoiced along with me.

49
SABBATICAL

"Your potential is my mission."

In late January, the same month I flew down to meet Allene and Sharon for the first time, Joan and I traveled to a suburb north of Philadelphia to meet my oldest sibling, Hester, and her family. We drove through a snowstorm to get there, but it was a great evening. Hester and her husband, Paul, were gracious hosts; we all pushed through the initial awkwardness until we found warmth, acceptance, and a genuine desire to know each other as family. Their two teen-aged daughters accepted me right away and even started calling me Uncle Bob. At the end of the evening, Paul suggested we stay the night, but we decided to drive back to our hotel. The snowstorm had blown and blustered all through dinner and our visit; a solid four to six inches covering the ground. On the slow drive back to our hotel, the time passed quickly as we reminisced about the evening.

Winter moved slowly into spring. My sisters and I shared a mutual interest in finding out more about our history and each other. We scheduled some times together to get better acquainted, and I sensed a level of trust growing in all of us. My own kids and their families traveled to meet my sisters. We started seeing each other at holidays and enjoyed a short vacation together so our extended families could spend time with each other. We visited each other's homes and discovered all sorts of similarities amongst ourselves.

Hester and I ordered our scrambled eggs the exact same way. All four of us had freckled skin just like our father, Drew. It felt like a new season of life. I heard a quote from the movie, *Broadcast News*, "My life has exceeded my dreams," and began using it. It felt completely true for me.

By now, I had been the District Superintendent of the Potomac District Assemblies of God for eight years. When I moved into the position, one of the goals I set was to visit every church, large or small, at least once during my tenure in Fairfax, Virginia. With 315 churches, most of my weekends were spent traveling to visit and speak. I started recognizing the clear signals that I needed a break. It was taking longer to recharge physically, emotionally, mentally, and spiritually after our annual conference, as well as after the tough meetings or decisions concerning a struggling pastor or congregation. While I was speaking most weekends at one of our churches, I was also invited to speak at conferences in other districts. The travel schedule added to my fatigue. I had been encouraging pastors to take a sabbatical to recalibrate every five to seven years. How could I ask them to follow this self-care if I didn't model what I was teaching?

The board granted me a six-week sabbatical and during that time I chose to visit some churches that were not Assemblies of God and observe what others were doing in worship style, preaching, hospitality, discipleship, and missions. I also met with several individuals who could speak wisdom into my life. Dr. Howard Hendricks, a professor at Dallas Theological Seminary and a recognized leader in mentoring, agreed to meet with me. I came away with pages of notes from my time with him. At one point in our meeting I asked Dr. Hendricks what he would say to ministers if he were in my position? Without hesitation he said, "I would look at each one and say, 'Your potential is my mission'!" That was the kairos moment of the entire sabbatical. That was the moment everything clicked into place because the Holy Spirit spoke and I listened at the exact same time.

I returned to my position and began speaking those words, "Your potential is my mission," to ministers everywhere I went. I pledged to do whatever I could to help each one reach their potential. I also asked them to think about their congregations. What if each Sunday they reminded the congregation that "your potential is my mission?" What if every sermon, every action, had that thought as its motivation? When God looks at us that is what he sees. That is what he says. He gave his Son and the Holy Spirit to help each of us reach our potential. The phrase caught momentum and for the remainder of my time as Superintendent that theme resonated throughout the Potomac District. Some of my colleagues grabbed the idea too and used it in their respective venues. I entered the second half of my 15 years invigorated and forging ahead with a clear vision. God was still invested in me. He knew me, intimately, and had whispered in my ear countless times during my life, "Your potential is my mission."

50
TRUST

"Bob, I had my doubts when I first met you.
I kept wondering, what does this preacher want?"

My brother-in-law, Buz, shared this with me one evening after
we had settled into a more comfortable relationship as extended
family. Buz was my youngest sister, Sharon's, husband and proved
to be the most skeptical at first. He didn't really trust me when I
entered the picture, but over time he saw that I just wanted to be
a brother. He and I grew to understand and respect each other.
Buz was a businessman and made his living in real estate and
development. Buz was savvy, smart, and a hard worker. It took him a
while to trust me, but once he trusted, Buz was all in. We could talk
about anything and challenged each other in many areas of life.

Buz had a remarkable faith story. He had considered himself
a Christian and was a member of a church, but after becoming
a millionaire by the age of 30, he felt empty inside and realized
his faith journey wasn't meaningful. His teenage daughter started
attending a different church and came home excited about her faith
with pages of notes she had taken from just one sermon. Buz and
Sharon were curious and noticed the impact the church was having
on their daughter. After a few weeks they decided to attend a service
with her and see for themselves what kind of church could generate
such enthusiasm for Christ. The service and minister were engaging

and they learned so much from one sermon that they went back the next week. Before long they were attending every week, and their own faith sprung to life and started growing.

I arranged for Buz to speak in chapel and in classes to business students at Valley Forge Christian College. I had some connections there and thought his faith journey as a businessman would be inspiring and helpful. He agreed to come and speak and the students were riveted as he told his story. When he was finished we drove back to Fairfax. Buz and Sharon were staying with us over the weekend and planned to do a little sight-seeing in Washington D.C. before heading back to Florida. On Saturday morning as I prepared to attend a District wide youth event to give a greeting, I had this idea to invite Buz to ride along. He readily agreed. I wasn't even sure why I invited him, but I recognized the nudging of the Holy Spirit. I knew that usually all we get is a small nudge and many times it's just to plant a seed, not reap a whole harvest of what God intends to nurture and grow.

While I was giving my greeting to the 2000 plus group of teenagers, Buz sat beside a missionary named Rick Caswell on the front row. Afterward Buz and Rick talked for quite a while and I realized Buz was very engaged in the conversation. Something was stirring in his heart. Rick shared with Buz his vision of building small churches in Mali for $5000 each. He had acquired land in Mali and was excited about the potential churches that could be built. But he wasn't getting the financial response he had expected from the states and was growing frustrated. His idea was to raise money for seven churches at a time and then ship the materials for those seven churches in a container from the U.S. Teams from different churches in the states would then travel to Mali and build the churches.

It was quiet on our drive back home and I wondered what Buz was thinking. A missionary's view of spending and profit was a little different than a businessman's.

"Was that guy for real?" Buz broke the silence with his straight forward question.

"Absolutely," I replied.

Buz was intrigued by the idea of raising money to build churches so far away and had connected, even empathized, with the frustration of having a golden opportunity that struggled due to lack of financial backing. I could tell he was mulling it over in his head. Finally he sighed and said, "I need to think some more about this."

A year later Buz called me one day and asked, "Is that missionary still building those churches?" A quick call to Rick confirmed he was. When I spoke to Buz again he said, " I've been thinking about that conversation I had with Rick. He seemed so discouraged. I've prayed about it and want to help. I just sold a property so I'd like to give some of the money to Rick."

"You want to buy the supplies to build a church?" I asked.

"No, I want to buy a whole container to build seven churches."

I almost dropped the phone as I struggled to gather my thoughts.

"On one condition," I said. "When the churches are finished you travel to Mali with me to see what God's done with your money."

He reluctantly agreed. Later I learned he simply agreed with no intention of going to Mali. The check for $35,000 arrived and Rick called it miracle money. The Holy Spirit's nudge to invite Buz to a youth convention led to a donation that funded seven new churches built in Mali.

Buz and I traveled together two years later to visit the churches and see the small towns and villages where the congregants lived. Buz went kicking and screaming. He had never been to Africa except on luxurious hunting trips and primarily in South Africa. The trip changed Buz. We slept under mosquito nets and visited five out of the seven churches. Buz teared up when he saw the churches. He experienced God and the Kingdom in a clear and meaningful way. I watched trust and understanding grow in Buz. He could trust that God was ever-present and cared for the whole world. He understood that all the riches in the world couldn't compare with God's extravagant love and boundless grace. Buz thought he was building churches, but more than that, God was building trust and relationship and purpose in Buz's heart.

After that trip Buz wanted to do more to support missionaries like Rick. By this time he owned and ran a restaurant called Squid Lips. With the restaurant profits, he founded Missionary Family Ministries, which provides evangelism resources to missionaries free of charge. He also put a prayer box in the restaurant lobby and encouraged customers to write down prayer concerns. He prayed over scraps of paper each week. Prayed for people he didn't even know, but he trusted that God knew and that was all that mattered. It was the beginning of a beautiful generosity. I learned later that the property Buz sold to fund the churches in Mali, was his own home. A beautiful home on beachfront property that he had lived in for over twenty years. He told me he couldn't stop thinking about Rick and those churches he wanted to build. Buz prayed about it and felt like God said to him, "There's a lot of equity in this house that I could use to build churches in Mali."

I marveled at how personal God can be with each of us. He knows exactly what we need and for how long. When one season ends, He has no problem beginning a new one just as full and rich as the last. I sensed God was signaling an end to my season as District Superintendent when I woke early one morning in August. I remember looking at the clock that read 5:37 a.m. and having the thought, *Trust me,* run through my head repeatedly. I didn't know what was coming next, but I knew I could trust God fully.

51
STILL

"Be still and know that I am God."
Psalm 46:10

I knew God wanted me to trust him at 62 with the same kind of faith I had at 26 when Joan and I started at WEAG. One would think trusting a God who has been faithful for six decades would come easily with no worries at all; but I found that trust, even in my sixties, had less to do with experience and more to do with obedience. Joan and I said good-bye to our season of serving the Potomac District, moved back to Richmond, and waited for a clear direction.

The next few years were difficult. The housing market hit an all-time low so we decided to rent rather than sell our home in Fairfax. During this time, our daughter, Julie, experienced a serious, life-threatening medical complication related to Crohn's disease. Joan and I spent weeks traveling back and forth from Virginia to Ohio to help her husband and young family as she recovered. There was no clear sign from God about moving forward into another ministry, only in being present and still. Anyone who knows me well knows I'm not good at being still. Why wasn't anything happening? I probably could have served longer as the District Superintendent, but distinctly felt God telling me it was time to step away from that season and start another. What was the next season? Was ministry over for me? I cried out to God privately and asked these very questions. I felt the undercurrent of uncertainty and it didn't have the same appeal as when I was in my twenties.

Trusting God can only be practiced in the midst of circumstances that actually require full trust. There is no expiration date or shelf life on trust; we are invited to live a life of trusting Him always; and even when we can't, we ask Him to help us trust. It was a real struggle some weeks, but God remained faithful in our stillness. Julie recovered and returned to raising a family and writing. Joan and I continued being still and asking God what was next for us. There were no bells or whistles. Just day to day living. Day to day growing. Day to day listening for God.

I started thinking about a dream I had been carrying in my heart for years - to create a special leadership experience for eight to ten University of Valley Forge students who were training to go into ministry. The dream moved from my heart to my head over the slow months and I began to puzzle it out. How would a leadership experience work? Who would fund it? What experiences would both support and challenge students planning to enter the ministry? Finally, I approached the administration at the University of Valley Forge and shared the idea. They loved it and together we began mapping out a time frame and process for selecting the students. A foundation agreed to fund the first year. Now I just had to plan the event.

I used all my connections in the Potomac District and Washington, D.C. area to pull together a comprehensive and thought-provoking mentoring experience for young, vibrant ministerial students. The voices of my own mentors from years past surfaced and I realized how much people like the Davises, Ira Stanphill, and David Wilkerson had greatly impacted my life of ministry. My professors at Toccoa had mentored me as well. I hoped to do the same for these college students.

During this time I got an unexpected phone call from a friend who asked if I would be interested in helping his church make a pastoral transition. Would I possibly consider serving as the interim pastor for a while? I didn't need to think about it. I didn't need to pray about it. I had already been thinking and praying every day, asking God what came next. Interim pastoring was something I'd never considered or pursued, but it made sense. I had pastored congregations. I had pastored pastors. I had walked many pastors and congregations through difficult seasons. Temporarily stepping in for a pastor seemed like the right next thing to do.

By the time I started making trips to Hampton, Virginia to serve as interim pastor for Bethel Temple Assembly of God, the first Innovative Leadership Experience I had been planning for Valley Forge students materialized. On a sunny, spring Wednesday in 2007, ten eager ministry students and myself boarded a small bus at noon and headed off to Washington, D.C. on an all-expense paid leadership experience. During the days we visited places like the Russell Senate building to meet a senator who was a Christ-follower and hear his story or tour the White House and Capital and visit the Justice Department to hear Attorney General Ashcroft challenge the students to give their best and be a leader others wanted to follow. We connected with Dick Foth and listened as he shared what he knew about leaders and the importance of relationships. We met with the Chaplain of the Senate, pastors, and businessmen. We visited a city church, a church practicing authentic race reconciliation, a church with a GenX-ers service that used ancient symbolic practices like lighting candles for prayer combined with contemporary music and weekly communion.

In the evenings we stayed in a nice hotel and ate around tables in classic establishments like Old Ebbitt Grill, where I got to know these ten students personally as we de-briefed and examined practical leadership principles through authentic conversation. The students seemed captivated and I made a mental note to pursue another Innovative Leadership Experience for ten more students as soon as I got home. As we headed back to campus each of the students reflected on the five days. Many felt like it would stand out as a highlight in their training.

Over the next five years we took a total of 50 students through five days of a similar Innovative Leadership Experience. Eventually the funding ran out, but the small streams of experience started in each of these students trickled deeply and made an impact. Stillness is a powerful thing. When we stop moving long enough to really be still, God can use us, work through us, mold us in a different kind of way. What if we could be still and know? He is God of all things, certain and uncertain.

52
FINISHING STRONG

"As for me, I will always have hope."
Psalm 71:14

Bethel in Hampton became the first of ten church congregations I helped transition over the next eight years. It was amazing how I would finish with one church and another would invite me to come. I served in Virginia, Pennsylvania, Ohio, Illinois, and Florida. Each congregation offered a weekly stipend that helped meet our needs and more. When our house in Fairfax finally sold we were grateful to have that out from under us, but marveled at how God cared for us no matter what.

I led each church through a process of fasting and praying for a new pastor along with a practical grid that included an individual's calling, character, competency, and chemistry to evaluate candidates. One day while I was serving as interim pastor in Joliet, Illinois, a pastor from Florida called to share that God had been stirring his heart to prepare for a season of change. I didn't know him, but he sounded authentic. After listening to my reader's digest description of the church, he asked if he could visit at his own expense and take a prayer walk around the church.

In all my years of serving churches in transition, I don't think I was ever so surprised by a request. Jim came a few weeks later and took his prayer walk. Afterward I gave him an official tour around the building and we ended with prayer in the sanctuary. No one else even knew he was coming. Jim just wanted to spend time in the space and talk to God about whether or not he should apply to be a pastoral candidate here. When he left that day I knew I had met the next pastor of this church. I scheduled him to be a guest preacher and to have lunch with the board members. I had already told them the story of how I met Jim. After Jim's sermon and lunch meeting the board moved quickly in vetting him and he was elected with almost 100% vote.

When I was interim pastor in Youngstown, Ohio a potential candidate and wife visited as guest preacher one Sunday. After the morning service they met for lunch with the board and visited; they tried to determine if God was speaking to them about being an official pastoral candidate for the position. Near the end of the meeting Rhonda, the wife, said, "I feel like we are on a wild goose chase!" We later learned that Rhonda was quiet by nature and rarely spoke in meetings. The couple left to catch a plane home. In the parking lot they heard a goose honk and watched it take off, fly once around the church building, return back to the parking lot and honk again. It struck both of them that they were watching their very own wild goose chase. But seeing the crazy goose return to the church parking lot strangely gave them a sense that they should prayerfully consider being pastoral candidates for the church in Youngstown. They have been faithfully serving that congregation since 2013.

If I have learned one thing in life, it is that God has a sense of humor. I started ministry at age nineteen on the streets of New York with David Wilkerson. In an interesting turn of events, my son, Rob, and I were recently able to serve together in short-term pastoral roles for a city ministry in Richmond. This ministry, much like Teen Challenge, provided homes for men and women struggling with addiction and/or abused by sexual trafficking. There were also two thrift stores and a small cafe that gave these men and women a way to work and learn responsibility. The food pantry and a bus ministry for kids in at risk neighborhoods served the community. It felt a little like I was finishing where I began. I know ministry is never finished, but working in ministry with my son felt like a satisfying finale.

I used to think life was lived in one continuous straight line of events. These days I am humbled and amazed to see how life moves forward, and then folds back on itself. A new event stirs an old feeling and creates a different perspective about a memory. Like patching a new piece of fabric up against an old piece, intricate patterns are discovered. Similarities noticed. Truths revealed. My restlessness as a child and young adult was the very thing God used to catapult me into all life had to offer; and in response to His overwhelming love for me, I offered myself to Him through ministry.

There is still work to be done, but I have made peace with so many of the questions I used to ponder about family, faith, and the future. Some were answered. Some are continuously being answered. And some will remain questions for the rest of my life here on earth. While restlessness will always be a part of my human nature, I find my heart comfortably reconciled with the "from" and "to" of my life. I understand how I fit in a family. I recognize my deep need for redemption and companionship in Jesus. I trust the future because I trust the nature of my Hope.

When Hope becomes a noun, the whole journey is possible.

*Bob and Joan
wedding picture,
January 1966*

*West End
Assembly of God,
First building*

208

To Bob Rhoden
With best wishes, Ronald Reagan

Meeting
President
Reagan and
Nancy Reagan

Thanks
Bill Clinton

Dr. Rhoden

Autographed name card from White House
breakfast with President Clinton

Sculpture of "Tongues of Fire"

Bob and his three sisters, Hester, Allene, and Sharon

The Rhoden family, "My life has exceeded my dreams"

LEANING ON MY STAFF

"Tell us two or three things you have learned about life and ministry" is a frequent question I am asked in seminars and conferences. So let me borrow a page from Jacob, Abraham's grandson, to share ten life-changing principles I try to live by. Hebrews 11:21 says Jacob blessed Joseph's sons as he was dying and worshipped as he leaned on his staff. The narrative passage for this idea is located in Genesis 47:31 and 48:1-2. Maybe in some small way these life lessons will bless you. For sure it is a time of worship for me as I lean on my staff and reflect on life with you.

1. Our past does not need to trap us; it can shape us.

Everybody has a "from" in their life. I am from Olustee, orphaned when I was two, raised in poverty by a loving grandmother. It's very tempting to get trapped in our memories and use our past as an alibi for not reaching the potential God created in each of us. The tragedy of the story of the talents in Matthew 25 is the servant with one talent buried it rather than investing and doubling it like the other servants did with their talents. Dreams are made of "what if" not "if only" questions.

2. If we do the natural God will do the supernatural.

The young lad gave his lunch, but after Jesus blessed it, five thousand people were fed. What if the young lad had not given his lunch? When we do what we can, we are teeing up the ball for God to hit it out of the park. The Bible is replete with stories illustrating this idea. Naaman dips in the Jordan and God heals him. The woman gathers up empty jars from her neighbors and God increases the little oil she has to miraculously fill all the jars. I filter my daily life actions through this idea.

3. Those who know us best should believe in us the most.

As a pastor this was important in our family. Am I the same person at home that I am in the pulpit? No one gets it right all the time, but our goal is to make sure those who know us best have a true narrative to work with. You can't drift into this; it must be intentional. Craig Groeschel says at the end of each podcast, "People will follow someone who is always real rather than someone who is always right."

4. I don't fear failure as much as I fear I might succeed in things that don't matter.

This is a paraphrase from Francis Chan in his book *Crazy Love*. In our culture, success is measured by how much money we make and how many people serve us; but in God's economy success is measured by how much we give away and how many people we serve. Jesus said "a man's life does not consist in the abundance of his possessions" (Luke 12:15). His mission statement is clear, "For even the Son of Man did not come to be served, but to serve, and to give his life as a ransom for many" (Mark 10:45). Our success at the end of life will be measured by faithfulness to our mission, not by the amount of things we have accumulated.

5. Hang out with people who are wiser and more skilled than you are.

I embrace the idea that the three to five people we are around the most significantly influence our thinking. In sports we want to play with someone more skilled because it pushes us to improve. So I must be intentional about the people I choose to be with. Everyone needs a Paul to teach them, a Barnabas to encourage them, and a Timothy to mentor. Proverbs 13:22 sums up this idea with, "He who walks with the wise grows wise, but a companion of fools suffers harm".

6. It generally takes longer than we think.

Our world is microwave driven. We want it now. Taking time for something to bake tries our patience. I always prefer quick. But life has taught me the lesson of "little by little." After forty years in the wilderness, you know the Children of Israel were hoping for a "microwave" occupation of the land of promise. But God said, "I will not drive out the enemy in a single year because the wild animals in the land would be too numerous for you. Little by little I will drive them out before you, until you have increased enough to take possession of the land." (Exodus 23:29-30) Our Heavenly Father is gracious to us as we learn to trust His pace. He really does know best!

7. Talking to God out loud, rather than just listening to myself, helps me navigate difficult situations.

When I am processing a difficult situation I find it helpful to speak about the matter. My sanctuary is taking a drive alone so I can talk about the matter out loud in prayer with God. He absorbs my questions. He hears my concerns. As I express my deepest thoughts to someone I can trust, it's amazing how my mind and heart calm in His presence so I can be open to His perspective. I am not suggesting that I always have a eureka moment, but it does start the process toward an answer. I believe and make every effort to practice Jeremiah 33:3, "Call to me and I will answer you and tell you great and unsearchable things you do not know." When I want to experience more than I know, I talk to God.

8. My priorities determine my capacity.

This quote from Andy Stanley expresses what I came to know as a young husband, father, and pastor. This experiment using two jars, the same amount of sand, and four rocks, will illustrate the point. If you put the sand in first and then the rocks, they will not fit. But if you put the four rocks in first and then the sand, they fit. For me the four rocks represent my priorities: God, spouse, children and work. The sand represents everything else I have to do every day. If I focus on my to do list and neglect my priorities, I cannot fit it all in. But if I focus on my priorities first, then there is enough capacity for everything. Jesus said, "But seek first his kingdom and his righteousness, and all these things will be given to you as well." (Matthew 6:33)

9. What's happening is not what's going on.

I was introduced to this catchy phrase by a colleague from North Carolina when I served as Superintendent of the Potomac District. It describes the life of Joseph in the Bible as well as others. When the obvious events of the moment or maybe even the years do not seem to fit the dream we believe is God's intended purpose for us, just wait it out and be faithful. Romans 8:28 will eventually kick in if we do not lose heart and give up. Joseph said to his brothers, "You intended to harm me, but God intended it for good...." (Genesis 50:20) I read stories in the Bible through this lens and also note confusing seasons in my own life by saying, "What's happening is not what's going on".

10. My life has exceeded my dreams.

This is an adaptation from a quote in the movie *Broadcast News*, an American romantic comedy-drama film written, produced and directed by James L. Brooks in 1987. This phrase describes my life: child of God, husband to a loving faithful wife of 54 plus years, father to three awesome children and their spouses, grandfather to eight wonderful grandchildren, brother to three amazing sisters and their families who I discovered in1995, and a grateful man for many friends who are treasures. I've enjoyed a ministry serving as pastor and denominational leader, authored a book, met two U.S. Presidents, earned a terminal professional academic degree in ministry, and much more than space will allow here. It was a phrase I used to sum up my life at a retirement celebration in 2006. My prayer for all as I conclude is the benediction I used for the 22 years I served as pastor of West End Assembly of God, "May the favor of the Lord our God rest upon us; establish the work of our hands...." (Psalm 90:17)

FINALLY, it's been a journey of hope from Granny Cobb to Pastor Bob!